D1386719

William Shakespeare

MEASURE FOR MEASURE

Edited with a Commentary by J. M. Nosworthy
Introduced and revised by Julia Briggs

PENGUIN BOOKS

PENGUIN BOOKS

Published by the Penguin Group

Penguin Books Ltd, 80 Strand, London WC2R ORL, England

Penguin Group (USA) Inc., 375 Hudson Street, New York, New York 10014, USA

Penguin Group (Canada), 90 Eglinton Avenue East, Suite 700, Toronto, Ontario, Canada M4P 2Y3
(a division of Pearson Penguin Canada Inc.)

Penguin Ireland, 25 St Stephen's Green, Dublin 2, Ireland (a division of Penguin Books Ltd)

Penguin Group (Australia), 250 Camberwell Road, Camberwell, Victoria 3124, Australia
(a division of Pearson Australia Group Pty Ltd)

Penguin Books India Pvt Ltd, 11 Community Centre, Panchsheel Park, New Delhi – 110 017, India

Penguin Group (NZ), cnr Airborne and Rosedale Roads, Albany, Auckland 1310, New Zealand
(a division of Pearson New Zealand Ltd)

Penguin Books (South Africa) (Pty) Ltd, 24 Sturdee Avenue, Rosebank, Johannesburg 2196, South Africa

Penguin Books Ltd, Registered Offices: 80 Strand, London WC2R ORL, England

www.penguin.com

This edition first published in Penguin Books 1969
Reissued, with small revisions, in the Penguin Shakespeare series 2005

This edition copyright © Penguin Books, 1969
Account of the Text and Commentary copyright © J. M. Nosworthy, 1969; revised by Julia Briggs, 2005
General Introduction and Chronology copyright © Stanley Wells, 2005
Introduction, The Play in Performance and Further Reading copyright © Julia Briggs, 2005

Set in 11.5/12.5 PostScript Monotype Fournier
Designed by Boag Associates
Typeset by Palimpsest Book Production Limited, Polmont, Stirlingshire
Printed in England by Clays Ltd, St Ives plc

Contents

General Introduction

Every play by Shakespeare is unique. This is part of his greatness. A restless and indefatigable experimenter, he moved with a rare amalgamation of artistic integrity and dedicated professionalism from one kind of drama to another. Never shackled by convention, he offered his actors the alternation between serious and comic modes from play to play, and often also within the plays themselves, that the repertory system within which he worked demanded, and which provided an invaluable stimulus to his imagination. Introductions to individual works in this series attempt to define their individuality. But there are common factors that underpin Shakespeare's career.

Nothing in his heredity offers clues to the origins of his genius. His upbringing in Stratford-upon-Avon, where he was born in 1564, was unexceptional. His mother, born Mary Arden, came from a prosperous farming family. Her father chose her as his executor over her eight sisters and his four stepchildren when she was only in her late teens, which suggests that she was of more than average practical ability. Her husband John, a glover, apparently unable to write, was nevertheless a capable businessman and loyal townsfellow, who seems to have fallen on relatively hard times in later life. He would have been brought up as a Catholic, and may have retained

Catholic sympathies, but his son subscribed publicly to Anglicanism throughout his life.

The most important formative influence on Shakespeare was his school. As the son of an alderman who became bailiff (or mayor) in 1568, he had the right to attend the town's grammar school. Here he would have received an education grounded in classical rhetoric and oratory, studying authors such as Ovid, Cicero and Quintilian, and would have been required to read, speak, write and even think in Latin from his early years. This classical education permeates Shakespeare's work from the beginning to the end of his career. It is apparent in the self-conscious classicism of plays of the early 1590s such as the tragedy of *Titus Andronicus*, *The Comedy of Errors*, and the narrative poems *Venus and Adonis* (1592–3) and *The Rape of Lucrece* (1593–4), and is still evident in his latest plays, informing the dream visions of *Pericles* and *Cymbeline* and the masque in *The Tempest*, written between 1607 and 1611. It inflects his literary style throughout his career. In his earliest writings the verse, based on the ten-syllabled, five-beat iambic pentameter, is highly patterned. Rhetorical devices deriving from classical literature, such as alliteration and antithesis, extended similes and elaborate wordplay, abound. Often, as in *Love's Labour's Lost* and *A Midsummer Night's Dream*, he uses rhyming patterns associated with lyric poetry, each line self-contained in sense, the prose as well as the verse employing elaborate figures of speech. Writing at a time of linguistic ferment, Shakespeare frequently imports Latinisms into English, coining words such as abstemious, addiction, incarnadine and adjunct. He was also heavily influenced by the eloquent translations of the Bible in both the Bishops' and the Geneva versions. As his experience grows, his verse and prose become more supple, the patterning less apparent, more ready to accommodate the rhythms of ordinary speech, more colloquial in diction, as in the speeches of the Nurse in *Romeo and Juliet*, the characterful prose of Falstaff and Hamlet's soliloquies. The effect is of increasing psychological realism, reaching its greatest heights in *Hamlet*, *Othello*, *King Lear*, *Macbeth* and *Antony and Cleopatra*. Gradually he discovered ways of adapting the regular beat of the pentameter to make it an infinitely flexible instrument for matching thought with feeling. Towards the end of his career, in plays such as *The Winter's Tale*, *Cymbeline* and *The Tempest*, he adopts a more highly mannered style, in keeping with the more overtly symbolical and emblematical mode in which he is writing.

So far as we know, Shakespeare lived in Stratford till after his marriage to Anne Hathaway, eight years his senior, in 1582. They had three children: a daughter, Susanna, born in 1583 within six months of their marriage, and twins, Hamnet and Judith, born in 1585. The next seven years of Shakespeare's life are virtually a blank. Theories that he may have been, for instance, a schoolmaster, or a lawyer, or a soldier, or a sailor, lack evidence to support them. The first reference to him in print, in Robert Greene's pamphlet *Greene's Groatsworth of Wit* of 1592, parodies a line from *Henry VI, Part III*, implying that Shakespeare was already an established playwright. It seems likely that at some unknown point after the birth of his twins he joined a theatre company and gained experience as both actor and writer in the provinces and London. The London theatres closed because of plague in 1593 and 1594; and during these years, perhaps recognizing the need for an alternative career, he wrote and published the narrative poems *Venus and Adonis* and *The Rape of Lucrece*. These are the only works we can be certain that Shakespeare himself was responsible for putting into print. Each bears the author's dedication to Henry Wriothesley, Earl of Southampton (1573–1624), the second in warmer terms than the first. Southampton, younger than Shakespeare by ten years, is the only person to whom he personally dedicated works. The Earl may have been a close friend, perhaps even the beautiful and adored young man whom Shakespeare celebrates in his *Sonnets*.

The resumption of playing after the plague years saw the founding of the Lord Chamberlain's Men, a company to which Shakespeare was to belong for the rest of his career, as actor, shareholder and playwright. No other dramatist of the period had so stable a relationship with a single company. Shakespeare knew the actors for whom he was writing and the conditions in which they performed. The permanent company was made up of around twelve to fourteen players, but one actor often played more than one role in a play and additional actors were hired as needed. Led by the tragedian Richard Burbage (1568–1619) and, initially, the comic actor Will Kemp (d. 1603), they rapidly achieved a high reputation, and when King James I succeeded Queen Elizabeth I in 1603 they were renamed as the King's Men. All the women's parts were played by boys; there is no evidence that any female role was ever played by a male actor over the age of about eighteen. Shakespeare had enough confidence in his boys to write for them long and demanding roles such as Rosalind (who, like other heroines of the romantic comedies, is disguised as a boy for much of the action) in *As You Like It*, Lady Macbeth and Cleopatra. But there are far more fathers than mothers, sons than daughters, in his plays, few if any of which require more than the company's normal complement of three or four boys.

The company played primarily in London's public playhouses – there were almost none that we know of in the rest of the country – initially in the Theatre, built in Shoreditch in 1576, and from 1599 in the Globe, on Bankside. These were wooden, more or less circular structures, open to the air, with a thrust stage surmounted by a canopy and jutting into the area where spectators who paid one penny stood, and surrounded by galleries where it was possible to be seated on payment of an additional penny. Though properties such as cauldrons, stocks, artificial trees or beds could indicate locality, there was no representational scenery. Sound effects such as flourishes of trumpets, music both martial and amorous, and accompaniments to songs were provided by the company's musicians. Actors entered through doors in the back wall of the stage. Above it was a balconied area that could represent the walls of a town (as in *King John*), or a castle (as in *Richard II*), and indeed a balcony (as in *Romeo and Juliet*). In 1609 the company also acquired the use of the Blackfriars, a smaller, indoor theatre to which admission was more expensive, and which permitted the use of more spectacular stage effects such as the descent of Jupiter on an eagle in *Cymbeline* and of goddesses in *The Tempest*. And they would frequently perform before the court in royal residences and, on their regular tours into the provinces, in non-theatrical spaces such as inns, guildhalls and the great halls of country houses.

Early in his career Shakespeare may have worked in collaboration, perhaps with Thomas Nashe (1567–*c*. 1601) in *Henry VI, Part I* and with George Peele (1556–96) in *Titus Andronicus*. And towards the end he collaborated with George Wilkins (*fl*. 1604–8) in *Pericles*, and with his younger colleagues Thomas Middleton (1580–1627), in *Timon of Athens*, and John Fletcher (1579–1625), in *Henry*

VIII, *The Two Noble Kinsmen* and the lost play *Cardenio*. Shakespeare's output dwindled in his last years, and he died in 1616 in Stratford, where he owned a fine house, New Place, and much land. His only son had died at the age of eleven, in 1596, and his last descendant died in 1670. New Place was destroyed in the eighteenth century but the other Stratford houses associated with his life are maintained and displayed to the public by the Shakespeare Birthplace Trust.

One of the most remarkable features of Shakespeare's plays is their intellectual and emotional scope. They span a great range from the lightest of comedies, such as *The Two Gentlemen of Verona* and *The Comedy of Errors*, to the profoundest of tragedies, such as *King Lear* and *Macbeth*. He maintained an output of around two plays a year, ringing the changes between comic and serious. All his comedies have serious elements: Shylock, in *The Merchant of Venice*, almost reaches tragic dimensions, and *Measure for Measure* is profoundly serious in its examination of moral problems. Equally, none of his tragedies is without humour: Hamlet is as witty as any of his comic heroes, *Macbeth* has its Porter, and *King Lear* its Fool. His greatest comic character, Falstaff, inhabits the history plays and *Henry V* ends with a marriage, while *Henry VI, Part III*, *Richard II* and *Richard III* culminate in the tragic deaths of their protagonists.

Although in performance Shakespeare's characters can give the impression of a superabundant reality, he is not a naturalistic dramatist. None of his plays is explicitly set in his own time. The action of few of them (except for the English histories) is set even partly in England (exceptions are *The Merry Wives of Windsor* and the Induction to *The Taming of the Shrew*). Italy is his favoured location. Most of his principal story-lines derive from printed writings; but the structuring and translation of these narratives into dramatic terms is Shakespeare's own, and he invents much additional material. Most of the plays contain elements of myth and legend, and many derive from ancient or more recent history or from romantic tales of ancient times and faraway places. All reflect his reading, often in close detail. Holinshed's *Chronicles* (1577, revised 1587), a great compendium of English, Scottish and Irish history, provided material for his English history plays. The *Lives of the Noble Grecians and Romans* by the Greek writer Plutarch, finely translated into English from the French by Sir Thomas North in 1579, provided much of the narrative material, and also a mass of verbal detail, for his plays about Roman history. Some plays are closely based on shorter individual works: *As You Like It*, for instance, on the novel *Rosalynde* (1590) by his near-contemporary Thomas Lodge (1558–1625), *The Winter's Tale* on *Pandosto* (1588) by his old rival Robert Greene (1558–92) and *Othello* on a story by the Italian Giraldi Cinthio (1504–73). And the language of his plays is permeated by the Bible, the Book of Common Prayer and the proverbial sayings of his day.

Shakespeare was popular with his contemporaries, but his commitment to the theatre and to the plays in performance is demonstrated by the fact that only about half of his plays appeared in print in his lifetime, in slim paperback volumes known as quartos, so called because they were made from printers' sheets folded twice to form four leaves (eight pages). None of them shows any sign that he was involved in their publication. For him, performance was the primary means of publication. The most frequently reprinted of his works were the non-dramatic poems – the erotic *Venus and Adonis* and the more moralistic *The Rape of Lucrece*. The *Sonnets*, which appeared in 1609, under his name but possibly without his consent, were less successful, perhaps because the vogue for sonnet sequences, which peaked in the 1590s, had passed by then. They were not reprinted until 1640, and then only in garbled form along with poems by other writers. Happily, in 1623, seven years after he died, his colleagues John Heminges (1556–1630) and Henry Condell (d. 1627) published his collected plays, including eighteen that had not previously appeared in print, in the first Folio, whose name derives from the fact that the printers' sheets were folded only once to produce two leaves (four pages). Some of the quarto editions are badly printed, and the fact that some plays exist in two, or even three, early versions creates problems for editors. These are discussed in the Account of the Text in each volume of this series.

Shakespeare's plays continued in the repertoire until the Puritans closed the theatres in 1642. When performances resumed after the Restoration of the monarchy in 1660 many of the plays were not to the taste of the times, especially because their mingling of genres and failure to meet the requirements of poetic justice offended against the dictates of neoclassicism. Some, such as *The Tempest* (changed by John Dryden and William Davenant in 1667 to suit contemporary taste), *King Lear* (to which Nahum Tate gave a happy ending in 1681) and *Richard III* (heavily adapted by Colley Cibber in 1700 as a vehicle for his own talents), were extensively rewritten; others fell into neglect. Slowly they regained their place in the repertoire, and they continued to be reprinted, but it was not until the great actor David Garrick (1717–79) organized a spectacular jubilee in Stratford in 1769 that Shakespeare began to be regarded as a transcendental genius. Garrick's idolatry prefigured the enthusiasm of critics such as Samuel Taylor Coleridge (1772–1834) and William Hazlitt (1778–1830). Gradually Shakespeare's reputation spread abroad, to Germany, America, France and to other European countries.

During the nineteenth century, though the plays were generally still performed in heavily adapted or abbreviated versions, a large body of scholarship and criticism began to amass. Partly as a result of a general swing in education away from the teaching of Greek and Roman texts and towards literature written in English, Shakespeare became the object of intensive study in schools and universities. In the theatre, important turning points were the work in England of two theatre directors, William Poel (1852–1934) and his disciple Harley Granville-Barker (1877–1946), who showed that the application of knowledge, some of it newly acquired, of early staging conditions to performance of the plays could render the original texts viable in terms of the modern theatre. During the twentieth century appreciation of Shakespeare's work, encouraged by the availability of audio, film and video versions of the plays, spread around the world to such an extent that he can now be claimed as a global author.

The influence of Shakespeare's works permeates the English language. Phrases from his plays and poems – 'a tower of strength', 'green-eyed jealousy', 'a foregone conclusion' – are on the lips of people who may never have read him. They have inspired composers of songs, orchestral music and operas; painters and sculptors; poets, novelists and film-makers. Allusions to him appear in pop songs, in advertisements and in television shows. Some of his characters – Romeo and Juliet, Falstaff, Shylock and Hamlet – have acquired mythic status. He is valued for his humanity, his psychological insight, his wit and humour, his lyricism, his mastery of language, his ability to excite, surprise, move and, in the widest sense of the word, entertain audiences. He is the greatest of poets, but he is essentially a dramatic poet. Though his plays have much to offer to readers, they exist fully only in performance. In these volumes we offer individual introductions, notes on language and on specific points of the text, suggestions for further reading and information about how each work has been edited. In addition we include accounts of the ways in which successive generations of interpreters and audiences have responded to challenges and rewards offered by the plays. The Penguin Shakespeare series aspires to remove obstacles to understanding and to make pleasurable the reading of the work of the man who has done more than most to make us understand what it is to be human.

Stanley Wells

The Chronology of Shakespeare's Works

A few of Shakespeare's writings can be fairly precisely dated. An allusion to the Earl of Essex in the chorus to Act V of *Henry V*, for instance, could only have been written in 1599. But for many of the plays we have only vague information, such as the date of publication, which may have occurred long after composition, the date of a performance, which may not have been the first, or a list in Francis Meres's book *Palladis Tamia*, published in 1598, which tells us only that the plays listed there must have been written by that year. The chronology of the early plays is particularly difficult to establish. Not everyone would agree that the first part of *Henry VI* was written after the third, for instance, or *Romeo and Juliet* before *A Midsummer Night's Dream*. The following table is based on the 'Canon and Chronology' section in *William Shakespeare: A Textual Companion*, by Stanley Wells and Gary Taylor, with John Jowett and William Montgomery (1987), where more detailed information and discussion may be found.

The Two Gentlemen of Verona	1590–91
The Taming of the Shrew	1590–91
Henry VI, Part II	1591
Henry VI, Part III	1591

Introduction

'*The web of our life is of a mingled yarn, good and ill together. Our virtues would be proud if our faults whipped them not, and our crimes would despair if they were not cherished by our virtues.*' (*All's Well That Ends Well*, IV.3.70–73)

THE TITLE

The title of *Measure for Measure* reflects its concern with notions of balance and counterbalance, argument and counter-argument, action and counter-action. The play sets individual freedom against the law, the heart against the head, mercy against justice, intention against action, and the conclusion, if any, must be that moral clarity is hard to come by, for there are many ways of looking at any question, and as attitudes and perspectives change from one person to the next, so does the nature of judgement. All of Shakespeare's plays are alive to the conflicts between different value systems, but this one is more alive to them than most.

Shakespeare took his title from the New Testament, from a text central to Christ's Sermon on the Mount, and one which occurs, with only small variations, in three of the gospels, Matthew, Mark and Luke. This is the version according to St Matthew:

Judge not, that ye be not judged. For with what judgment ye judge, ye shall be judged: and with what measure ye mete, it shall be measured to you again. (Matthew 7:1–2)

These words occur within a discussion of the need for love and forgiveness, even towards enemies. They reject the older law of Moses and the Old Testament which had promised the justice of revenge or retribution (the so-called 'lex talionis'), the strict justice expressed in 'an eye for an eye, and a tooth for a tooth'. According to that old law, anything that was taken from another, damaged or destroyed had to be repaid and restored in full, as far as was possible. Yet the wording of Christ's command, while warning against the condemnation of others, itself suggests just such a retributive justice as its context clearly contradicts, and this is particularly true of the wording of this passage in St Luke's version: 'for with what measure ye mete, with the same shall men mete to you again' (6:38).

The ambiguity of these words was obvious to Shakespeare, and he exploited it in his early history play, *Henry VI, Part III*, itself a sequence of revenges and re-taliations, at the point when Warwick the King-Maker is about to decapitate the dying Lancastrian, Clifford. He tells his fellow Yorkists,

> From off the gates of York fetch down the head,
> Your father's head, which Clifford placèd there;
> Instead whereof let this supply the room:
> Measure for measure must be answerèd. (II.6.52–5)

It may be no more than coincidence that at the centre of the action of *Measure for Measure* occurs another, and rather different, exchange of heads. Thus, while apparently repudiating the Old Testament system of punishments to fit the crime, from another point of view, the doctrine of 'Measure for Measure' also seems to reassert it: if you judge, if you measure, expect to be judged and measured yourself. St Matthew's words recall a principle that existed under Roman (though never under English) law, recorded in the Digest of Justinian: if you punish someone for a sin you commit yourself, you are liable to suffer the same punishment.

There is a second and more general problem present in these words from the gospel, making them an appropriate starting point for a play of complex moral dilemmas, for if there is to be no judging of others, does that mean that there can be no shared law? Most communities require their members to conform to a set of shared laws in order to live in peace and function as communities. Without judgement – and therefore, without law – can the community, the state (whether that of Shakespeare's England or of his imaginary Vienna), continue to exist? Elizabethan theologians were well aware of this difficulty and insisted that this passage was concerned only with private judgement – it did not affect the duties of magistrates and governors, to rule, judge and punish, as God's representatives on earth. One commentator felt obliged to add that 'the wicked Anabaptists [the anarchists of Shakespeare's day] are to be banished which condemn temporal or civil judgments' (quoted by Pope, *Shakespeare Survey 2*, p. 259). *Measure for Measure* offers a sustained exploration of the meaning of these words from the gospel. Before the play is over, it will invoke a sense of the tyranny, absurdity and pathos of 'man . . . Dressed in a little brief authority' (II.2.117–18), and call in question the hierarchic structure of Shakespeare's society, as well as the power and privilege of its great ones.

The play begins with the Duke of Vienna retiring from office, leaving his deputy Angelo to rule in his place, in the hope that Angelo will tighten up the city's laws. These have fallen into disuse, and prostitution and sexually transmitted disease have become widespread. In an effort to reduce these problems, Angelo revives an old law that punishes with death all sex acts outside marriage. When Claudio, a well-brought-up young man soon to be married, gets his fiancée Juliet pregnant, Angelo rules that he must be executed, as an example to others. His fellow judge, Escalus, pleads for Claudio's life, asking Angelo 'Whether you had not sometime in your life | Erred in this point which now you censure him'. Angelo replies,

> When I, that censure him, do so offend,
> Let mine own judgement pattern out my death
> And nothing come in partial. (II.1.14–15, 29–31)

In other words, if Angelo commits the same crime as Claudio, he would expect the same punishment. He doesn't realize how close he is to doing so.

At Claudio's request, his sister Isabella, about to become a nun, goes to the deputy to plead for her brother's life. As she makes her case for him, drawing on a range of ethical and religious arguments, Angelo becomes deeply aroused by her and proposes the 'monstrous bargain': if she agrees to have sex with him, he will save her brother's life. Now, it seems, Angelo is about to commit the crime for which Claudio has been condemned to death – but is it the same crime? Blackmailing Isabella into sleeping with him looks far worse, morally speaking, than merely anticipating marriage, as Claudio and Juliet have done – for, as Juliet agrees, their 'most offenceful act | Was mutually committed' (II.3.26–7).

At this point, the Duke has returned, disguised as a friar, to see what has been going on in his absence. He now saves the situation by substituting Angelo's old fiancée Mariana for Isabella. Angelo had abandoned her when her dowry was lost at sea, but she is still mourning for his lost love. If Mariana takes Isabella's place, and lets Angelo have sex with her in the dark, no one will be any the wiser, and Claudio's life will be saved. But to the Duke's horror, Angelo refuses to keep his side of the bargain: instead, he sends a messenger to the prison in the small hours to demand that Claudio be executed and his head immediately sent back to him. Once again, the Duke secretly saves the day, and then goes on to stage a grand public entry to the city, this time dressed as himself.

In the long final scene, Isabella denounces Angelo to the Duke, and is in turn arrested for slandering his deputy. The Duke appears first as himself, and then in his disguise as a friar, only to be publicly exposed as the Duke. Now he promises Angelo the death to which Angelo had condemned Claudio:

'An Angelo for Claudio, death for death!'
Haste still pays haste, and leisure answers leisure,
Like doth quit like, and Measure still for Measure . . .
We do condemn thee to the very block
Where Claudio stooped to death, and with like haste.
    (V.1.406–8, 411–12)

Yet even as he speaks, the audience knows that, despite what Angelo and Isabella have been led to believe, Claudio has *not*, in fact, been executed on any block – and if Angelo is to be executed 'on the very block | Where Claudio stooped to death' (V.1.411–12), he won't actually be executed at all. In *Measure for Measure*, what actually happens, and what the various characters on stage think is happening, are often quite different, perhaps with the ultimate reminder that all these events are being played upon a stage, and thus to some extent are being acted out in our imagination – inside our heads.

HEADS, OR HEARTS?

'Head' is a key word and a key concept within the play. The rape of Isabella and the execution of Claudio, though threatened, remain no more than fantasies; they take place only inside Angelo's head. But the word 'head' signifies more than the mind or the imagination: in a properly regulated individual, the head should rule over the body, according to Renaissance ways of thinking. And that idea was extended from the individual to the state, where the 'head' – in this case, the Duke – is expected to rule over the body of the state, the people of Vienna. But in *Measure for Measure*, heads of all kinds are subject to a series of replacements and substitutions, beginning with the substitution of the deputy, Angelo, for the Duke as 'head' of Vienna, and followed by Angelo's blackmailing proposal to Isabella that she ransom her brother Claudio's head, forfeit to the old law, by yielding to him her own 'maiden head', that is, her virginity. And once that substitution has been promised, Angelo is anxious to cover his tracks by actually beheading Claudio (presumably so that he cannot afterwards be accused of accepting bribes). This results in a further complication in the plot, since Angelo does not merely refuse to keep his promise to Isabella to reprieve Claudio (a promise that the disguised Duke seems confident he will keep), but he insists on receiving Claudio's severed head, ordering it to be cut off four hours before the promised time (and thus either while he is keeping his assignation with Isabella, or immediately afterwards).

In the panic that follows, the Provost of the prison attempts and fails to persuade a convicted murderer, Barnadine, to be executed, so that his head might be substituted for Claudio's, and Claudio is only saved by the convenient offstage death of Ragozine ('a most notorious pirate', IV.3.69), who (equally conveniently) resembles Claudio, and whose head is therefore duly dispatched to the deputy, instead of Claudio's. Meanwhile the substitution of severed heads ('the head-trick') is closely paralleled by the substitution of maiden heads in Angelo's bed ('the bed-trick'), so that the deputy is now doubly deceived, believing that he possesses the severed head of Claudio (actually, Ragozine's), and that he has taken the maiden head of Isabella (actually, that of his ex-fiancée Mariana). And further, by sexually fulfilling his promised marriage to Mariana, it seems that he has legally become her husband, at any rate, according to the English laws of Shakespeare's day. Thus the exchanges or substitutions of heads make up the main action of the plot, while the rule of the 'head' over the rest of the body, both personal and political, is exactly the problem with which the play begins, as the Duke seeks to impose better regulation on Vienna through the rule of the harsher and supposedly more disciplined figure of Angelo. Angelo's failure to rule over his own desires, to make the head rule the rebellious or insubordinate body, makes him the play's central example of a human being on trial, laying him open to being judged as he has judged, to being punished with the same sentence as he has passed on Claudio.

At the same time, Angelo's case also demonstrates the inadequacy of any simple opposition between head and body, or between head and 'codpiece' (the part of dress that concealed men's genitals), between self-control and sexual desire. For Angelo's transgressive sexual desire itself sprang up from and was sustained by his imagination, as the play's action reveals, so that, from the very beginning, public rule as well as personal self-control are shown to be troubled at, or in, the head.

In addition to this head/body opposition, there was a further traditional opposition between 'head' and 'heart', the head being associated with rational conduct and the careful balancing of equity and justice (often demanded during the play, and particularly in the final scene), whereas the heart was the source of mercy and forgiveness, the spirit of the New Testament and the incarnation of Christ, who died to bring mercy to fallen mankind – as Isabella points out to Angelo in a speech that stands both morally and literally at the centre of the play:

> Alas, alas;
> Why, all the souls that were were forfeit once,
> And He that might the vantage best have took
> Found out the remedy. How would you be,
> If He, which is the top of judgement, should
> But judge you as you are? O think on that,
> And mercy then will breathe within your lips,
> Like man new made. (II.2.72–9)

Angelo responds to her argument by replying, 'It is the law, not I, condemn your brother', but it is soon to become painfully obvious that the laws are subject to manipulation by those in authority, and that the head of state may indeed break the state's laws and almost get away with it. The only record of a performance of *Measure for Measure* during Shakespeare's lifetime was before King James, the official patron of Shakespeare's acting troupe, at court on St Stephen's Day, 26 December 1604, as part of the Christmas festivities in the first year of the new king's reign. There was to be much debate in Parliament during James's reign as to how far the king could take the existing laws of the kingdom into his own hands and override them, or whether he was just as subject to them as every other individual. Some forty years on, his son Charles I would be arrested and beheaded over the same issue.

The play's argument between justice and mercy partly echoes that of the trial scene in *The Merchant of Venice*, written around seven years earlier (1596–7). It is the subject of Portia's famous speech that begins,

> The quality of mercy is not strained,
> It droppeth as the gentle rain from heaven
> Upon the place beneath. (IV.1.181–3)

Both Portia's and Isabella's pleas for mercy rather than strict justice are heart-stopping moments; both are spoken by women, as if behind them lay a tradition of female intercession that culminated in the Virgin Mary interceding with God, on behalf of the human soul. A debate between 'heart' and 'head' had already figured in *The Merchant of Venice*, in the words of the song sung while Bassanio made his choice of caskets at Belmont:

> Tell me where is Fancy bred,
> Or in the heart, or in the head?
> How begot, how nourishèd?
> Reply, reply. (III.2.63–6)

The reply given is that 'It is engendered in the eyes' (67), but the question of the origin of 'fancy' (desire) is linked with both heart and head, anticipating the play's later debate between mercy and justice, which can also be read as a debate between heart and head. Fancy (or fantasy) in Shakespeare's plays tends to be closely linked with the imagination. As Orsino says in the opening scene of *Twelfth Night*, 'So full of shapes is fancy, | That it alone is high fantastical' (14–15; desire is so full of imagination, that it is 'uniquely and supremely imaginative'), while in *A Midsummer Night's Dream* Theseus observes

> Lovers and madmen have such seething brains,
> Such shaping fantasies, that apprehend
> More than cool reason ever comprehends. (V.1.4–6)

The role of the imagination in engendering sexual desire (the breeding of 'fancy' in the 'head') is centrally embodied in Angelo's perverse response to Isabella's plea for Claudio. The city of Vienna, where

> liberty plucks justice by the nose;
> The baby beats the nurse, and quite athwart
> Goes all decorum (I.3.29–31)

repels him, with its suburbs seething with punks and pimps, 'but this virtuous maid | Subdues me quite' (II.2.185–6). His immediate reaction is to suspect her of

deliberately and deviously intending to arouse him:
'What's this? What's this? Is this her fault or mine? |
The tempter, or the tempted, who sins most?' (162–3)
But as his thoughts unwind, he begins to recognize that
it is her very chastity and modesty that draws him, and
makes him desire to violate her (as it draws Bertram to
Diana in *All's Well That Ends Well*, Iachimo to Imogen
in *Cymbeline* and Tarquin to Lucrece in Shakespeare's
poem *The Rape of Lucrece*):

> Can it be
> That modesty may more betray our sense
> Than woman's lightness? Having waste ground enough,
> Shall we desire to raze the sanctuary
> And pitch our evils there? O fie, fie, fie!
> What dost thou? Or what art thou, Angelo?
> Dost thou desire her foully for those things
> That make her good?' (168–75)

It is Isabella's difference from the general run of women,
and her determined resistance, that inspires his trans-
gressive desire to 'raze the sanctuary | And pitch our
evils there' (171–2, where 'evils' has both its usual sense
of wrongdoing, and the particular meaning of 'lavato-
ries', making it a disgustingly vivid image of the de-
secration of holy places). It is in part because Isabella is
on the point of becoming a nun that Angelo desires to
violate her; what is lacking in her (desire, or perhaps
feminine self-display) strongly engages his imagination.
The notion that goodness may draw evil to it, in some
inexplicable way, or even make good men evil is deeply
troubling, in general as well as in this particular instance,
and as much to the audience as to Angelo himself. While
his very name suggests an innate virtue, all Christians

knew the story of Lucifer's pride, and that 'Angels are bright still though the brightest fell' (*Macbeth*, IV.3.22). Angelo's name takes on ironic overtones that both he and others play upon: the Duke wonders, 'O, what may man within him hide, | Though angel on the outward side?' (III.2.259–60).

Angelo is only the most extreme example of the play's several double identities, the fallen angel who, having once strayed from the path of virtue, abandons himself almost eagerly to treachery, lies and deceptions. Whatever it was that he felt for Isabella does not inhibit him from cheating her over their bargain, dismissing her as a mad woman and watching her wrongfully arrested. But he is not the only character to display such inconsistencies: Lucio first appears as a loyal and helpful friend to Claudio, but later refuses to bail out his old accomplices, Pompey and Mistress Overdone, even though she has been supporting his child by Kate Keepdown. He also slanders the Duke (or so we must assume). According to Escalus, the Duke was one that 'contended especially to know himself . . . a gentleman of all temperance' (III.2.222–3, 227), whereas according to Lucio, he secretly indulged in sexual misbehaviour and that explained his lenience to others on that account: 'He had some feeling of the sport. He knew the service, and that instructed him to mercy' (III.2.113–14).

'OF WHAT DISPOSITION WAS THE DUKE'?

What, if anything, are we to make of Lucio's accusations? The Duke is the play's most enigmatic character, since 'we can approve his behaviour at the end of the play only at the cost of condemning his behaviour at the outset' (Nuttall, *Shakespeare Studies* 4, p. 239). His opening words announce (if somewhat obscurely) his concern with 'the properties of government', and he informs Friar Thomas that his motive for retiring from office is that during fourteen – or should it be nineteen? – years of rule (see I.2.167 and I.3.21), the laws have fallen into disuse and are now 'more mocked than feared' (I.3.7). In starting afresh, with no established reputation, the strict Lord Angelo will stand a better chance of making them work – whereas if the Duke had attempted the task himself it would have smacked of 'tyranny'. At the same time, the Duke intends to observe how Angelo conducts himself in his new position, and so find out whether he is really as upright as he seems. Angelo's first step had been to reintroduce the death penalty for sexual offences outside marriage in an attempt to clean up the city, the task that the Duke had appointed him to carry out. Yet by the end of the play, the Duke seems to have forgotten his earlier intentions, and the play ends with a public demonstration of forgiveness for all, described by A. D. Nuttall as 'an orgy of clemency' (*Shakespeare Studies* 4).

One solution to this inconsistency has been to see the ending as carrying the central message of the play, to read it as an example of the Christian forgiveness that is the central theme of the Sermon on the Mount (from which, as we have seen, Shakespeare took his title). The Duke can be seen to resemble God in his mercy as well as in the trials he imposes on individuals (since he tests Isabella, as well as Angelo); or if not quite God, then at least a figure of Christian Providence (the workings of God's purposes on earth), or else as God's earthly representative (as Renaissance rulers claimed to be). At the

climax of the play, when Lucio *'pulls off the Friar's hood,
and discovers the Duke'*, Angelo's response makes this sort
of comparison explicit:

> O my dread lord,
> I should be guiltier than my guiltiness
> To think I can be undiscernible,
> When I perceive your grace, like power divine,
> Hath looked upon my passes. (V.1.363–7)

The Duke appears to see himself as administering
Christian justice when he speaks of his spiritual respon-
sibilities in a soliloquy that stands out from the rest of
the play. It is composed, not in prose or blank verse (that
is, in unrhymed iambic pentameter), but in rhyming
couplets and iambic tetrameters, using a gnomic voice
that suggests widely acknowledged truths:

> He who the sword of heaven will bear
> Should be as holy as severe;
> Pattern in himself to know,
> Grace to stand, and virtue go. (III.2.249–52)

The Duke's judgements at the end have seemed to echo
those of Christ's parables in the New Testament, and the
Duke himself can be seen as an example of a teacher,
and a godly prince. Such interpretations strongly influenced a number of stage performances of the Duke, from
1930 onwards (when G. Wilson Knight first proposed this
interpretation). Such an account of the Duke may help
to reconcile audiences to Isabella's acceptance of his
marriage proposal (never made explicit in the text), since
her surrender of her vocation as a nun (a bride of Christ)
might seem less drastic if she is seen to be marrying

God's steward on earth. At the same time, his proposal itself suggests yet another inconsistency, since the Duke had claimed at the outset that he was not given to the softer emotions: 'Believe not that the dribbling dart of love | Can pierce a complete bosom' (I.3.2–3).

But for many critics, such an explanation lets the Duke off too lightly: far from actually being God or even his worthy representative, he is merely pretending, playing at being God. In that case, his testing of his subjects becomes distasteful, and his sense of justice flippant. For William Empson, the play expresses the view that 'the whole business of public justice is fatuous and hideous, whether compared to the mercy of Christ or the humanity of private life' ('*Sense* in *Measure for Measure*', *Structure of Complex Words*). From this perspective, the Duke's conduct during the course of the play is highly questionable, and his schemes morally dubious: his substitution of Mariana for Isabella in Angelo's bed can hardly be considered an honourable solution from anyone's point of view (even Mariana's), and his attempt to save Claudio by beheading Barnadine collapses altogether when Barnadine refuses to cooperate. Nor is it clear that it is permissible for a lay person to dress up as a friar and hear confession and prepare a condemned man for death. And, indeed, the Duke turns out to be scarcely better at theological instruction than he is at anticipating Angelo's reactions. His advice to Claudio, 'Be absolute for death' (III.1.5), far from offering spiritual consolation, turns into a series of secular reflections on the weariness of life, particularly unsuited to his young listener. Taken all in all, his behaviour lacks moral discrimination. One critic, A. P. Rossiter, thought that the Duke showed less charity and fellow-feeling for others than had Shakespeare's contemporary, the

Renaissance philosopher Michel de Montaigne.

And finally, the Duke's display of mercy at the play's end, the very gesture that seemed to reflect the gospel teachings most clearly, has been judged inappropriate. Sir Thomas Elyot in *The Boke named the Governour* (1531), an influential humanist account of 'the properties of government', advised his readers to distinguish between true mercy and 'vain pity | . . . wherein is contained neither justice nor yet commendable charity, but rather ensueth negligence, contempt, disobedience, and finally all mischief and incurable misery'. Both Escalus and Angelo recognize that justice has not only to be done, but must also be seen to be done. The Duke's inconsistent behaviour poses further problems: he 'entertains no worries about the rightness of pardoning [Barnadine] in Act 5 whom he was fully prepared to execute in Act 4: if the pardon is proper, the execution would have been a legal (but "damnable") murder', Graham Bradshaw observes (in *Shakespeare's Scepticism*, pp. 173–4). At this point, we may recall those Elizabethan theologians who insisted that the instruction against judging others at Matthew 7:1 only applied to private judgements, and in no way excused judges, rulers and governors from their obligation to judge and determine on behalf of the law and the state.

Though the Duke's dressing up as a friar is unusual, the story of the ruler who disguises himself to observe the vices or virtues of his people is a very ancient one, as old as the *Arabian Nights*, and older. Shakespeare may have had in mind the legend of the Roman Emperor Severus, who set out to cleanse his kingdom, using both public denunciation and private investigation. The ruler in disguise was, in any case, a popular figure in contemporary drama, used by Marston in *The Fawn* (*c.* 1605) and

The Malcontent (1602–4) and by Middleton in *The Phoenix* (1603–4) – indeed it became such a dramatic cliché that Ben Jonson parodied the device in *Bartholomew Fair* (1614), where Proctor Littlewit disguises himself to spy upon the 'follies of the fair'. Shakespeare's Henry V disguised himself to find out how his men were feeling on the eve of Agincourt. The ruler committed to improving the morals of his people also figured in protestant ideology as the godly prince, the status to which both Queen Elizabeth and King James aspired, though in very different ways. As patron of Shakespeare's company, the new king would have exerted an influence on Shakespeare's play, which was performed in his presence. Particular passages in the play seem to be borrowed from King James's recently published guide to politics and ethics, the *Basilikon Doron* (1599, 1603). The Duke's advice to Angelo in the opening scene draws on images from it:

> Heaven doth with us as we with torches do,
> Not light them for themselves: for if our virtues
> Did not go forth of us, 'twere all alike
> As if we had them not. (I.1.32–5)

And Escalus's account of the Duke's self-knowledge and temperance (quoted above) also corresponds to virtues that James particularly valued. Like the Duke, James felt that he had begun his reign too slackly, and on occasion during the first year of his rule, had indulged himself in a public display of mercy at the very last minute. Like the Duke, James might have claimed, 'I love the people, | But do not like to stage me to their eyes' (I.1.67–8), and he is echoed by Angelo at II.4.24–30 – both passages are thought to allude to a particular incident in March 1604, when James had intended to visit the Royal Entry decorations incognito, found himself overwhelmed by crowds struggling to catch a glimpse of him, and had been forced to take refuge in the Royal Exchange (according to Gilbert Dugdale in *The Time Triumphant*, 1604).

One further role sometimes attributed to the Duke is that of the playwright at work within the play – a part comparable to that of Prospero in *The Tempest*, of Iago in *Othello*, or even (passing from the sublime to the ridiculous) of Peter Quince in *A Midsummer Night's Dream* – it has even been suggested that Shakespeare might have played the Duke himself. It is true that the Duke organizes his own departure and secret return, and later sets up countermeasures to offset Angelo's evil initiatives, yet the limits of his power are exposed when he attempts to save Claudio's life by sacrificing Barnadine's. From almost every point of view, Barnadine is Claudio's antithesis: he is a foreigner rather than a respected citizen, a prisoner of long standing who has admitted that he is guilty of murder. Unlike Claudio, he shows no fear of death nor any wish for spiritual advice as death approaches. He spends most of his time drunk and, during his nine years' imprisonment, has apparently become institutionalized, rather than desiring freedom. The loss of his life would scarcely affect the community, whereas Claudio is urgently needed to support Juliet and her child. For all these reasons, he would seem to be the obvious person to die in Claudio's place.

But Barnadine refuses, point-blank, to do so: 'I have been drinking hard all night and I will have more time to prepare me, or they shall beat out my brains with billets' (IV.3.51–3). When the Duke insists, he refuses to listen and stalks back to his cell: 'If you have anything to say to me, come to my ward, for thence will not I today'

(60–61). Barnadine's intransigence, his refusal to 'die today for any man's persuasion' (57–8) represents the limits of the Duke's authority, whether as playwright within the play, as Friar (and spiritual adviser) or as the supreme head of state in Vienna. And Barnadine's refusal also places a limit on the powers of persuasion in a play where individual characters employ all the arts of language to bring others into line and to make them act as they would wish. It is Shakespeare's particular insight that Barnadine's power depends on his lack of status, as an outsider with no investment in the city's values. He can refuse the Duke point-blank precisely because he has nothing to lose. There is a paradoxical power in his extreme powerlessness and isolation, freed from the web of communal ties and duties that binds the rest of the characters. He remains as a surprising reminder that 'there is a world elsewhere'.

'NEITHER MAID, WIDOW, NOR WIFE?'

If Barnardine is an outsider, not merely to Vienna but almost to the human race itself, his position is not entirely unlike that of the play's three women characters, who in different ways are alienated or marginalized. In Shakespeare's day, women's status was defined in terms of marriage, as can be seen from the Duke's cross-questioning of the veiled Mariana in the final scene. He asks her whether she is a maid (waiting to be married), a wife or a widow, and when she denies being any of these, he replies, 'Why, you are nothing then. Neither maid, widow, nor wife?' (V.i.177–8). 'Nothing' or 'nought'(y) implied sexual misbehaviour. By rejecting the categories proposed, Mariana defined herself as sexually experienced, a maid who has lost the virginity she should have kept for her husband. Lucio enlarges upon the point: 'My Lord, she may be a punk. For many of them are neither maid, widow, nor wife' (179–80). By acknowledging her lack of recognized status, Mariana almost forfeits her right to a serious hearing, since marriage was women's expected destiny. 'All are understood either married or to be married', explained a law book of 1632. Women's status was defined within marriage, and it was the main determinant of their lives, so Mariana, the rejected fiancée, and Mistress Overdone, the 'punk' (or prostitute), are banished from polite society, while Isabella exemplifies another awkward possibility – that a young woman might not want to get married, since she intends to become a nun (an option not open to the women of Shakespeare's England, where the convents had all been closed by the Protestant Reformation).

Perhaps Mistress Overdone is the best equipped of the three to cope with her situation, for though she is arrested and sent to prison, it looks as if she may succeed in starting up her old business again from there – certainly Pompey announces, 'I am as well acquainted here as I was in our house of profession. One would think it were Mistress Overdone's own house, for here be many of her old customers' (IV.3.1–4). But Mariana's plight, abandoned in her moated grange (so vividly recreated in Tennyson's poem 'Mariana'), is a sad one, and Isabella's first response to the Duke's account of her is that she would be better off dead: 'What a merit were it in death to take this poor maid from the world!' (III.1.233–4). Isabella herself is also exceptional in her sense of vocation, a young woman who knows what she wants to do with her life. Angelo's proposal thus creates a cruel dilemma for her, and her decision – 'More than our brother is our chastity' (II.4.185) – has often lost her the sympathy of readers and audiences. In the past, her refusal to sacrifice herself for her brother would have been regarded as selfish and anti-social, since women were expected to put the needs of their male relatives before their own; in any case, true charity or love demanded that she set his life before her mere virginity. More recently, since the loss of virginity has become less significant in Western society, her refusal has once again seemed hard to understand, though this time for a different reason. But she had already given her reply to Angelo:

> Better it were a brother died at once
> Than that a sister, by redeeming him,
> Should die for ever. (II.4.106–8)

And, as she quite truthfully assures Claudio,

> O, were it but my life,
> I'd throw it down for your deliverance
> As frankly as a pin. (III.1.107–9)

It is Isabella's spiritual life that is at stake – her actions and words only be understood in the context of the seventeenth-century belief in an eternal afterlife, and the physical resurrection of the body after death (as we shall soon hear, Claudio pictures the afterlife he dreads as a series of appalling *physical* sensations, 121 ff.).

It has been further argued that her decision was the right one from a pragmatic point of view, since bargains cannot be made with evil-doers (as the play itself demonstrates, when Angelo fails to keep his side of the bargain). But worldly or prudential arguments of this kind play no part in her decision. Isabella's clear sense of self-determination is evident, both here and in her compensatingly generous decision to join Mariana in pleading for Angelo's life. Being a young woman who knows her own mind, Isabella's silence in response to the Duke's proposals near the end (V.1.489, 534) is unexpected, though it may be considered as one of several such 'open' silences. Perhaps in a Jacobean performance, the actors would break into a dance as the play ended, giving the audience little opportunity to dwell on its possible significance. In Shakespeare's age, Isabella would have been expected to accept the Duke's authority and his offer, although Beatrice, in *Much Ado About Nothing*, gracefully turns down Don Pedro's comparable proposal. In modern productions, Isabella's response to the Duke, and the audience reaction to it, will depend on how the Duke has been interpreted – the stronger his spiritual authority, the easier it is for an audience to accept him as a suitable husband for Isabella; but if he has been portrayed as an essentially secular figure, his request will recall Angelo's earlier demands, and Isabella may be seen as trapped and tormented by the agents of patriarchy.

HEAD-TRICKS, OR BED-TRICKS?

Isabella's rejection of Angelo's proposal, and Barnadine's refusal to die, both moments of great excitement though in very different ways, are among Shakespeare's major changes to his source material. As usual, he began with a number of versions of the story of the 'monstrous bargain', overlaying these with further folk or fairy-tale motifs, such as the legend of the disguised ruler, and the bed-trick. The story of the corrupt magistrate is an ancient one, going back at least to St Augustine (354–430), but a later version of it began to circulate in 1547: it was supposed to have taken place near Lake Como, during the rule of Frederic Gonzaga, Duke of Ferrara. A wife pleading with a magistrate for her husband's life, agreed to his sexual demands only to have him break his word and execute her husband. In the enquiry that followed, the magistrate was ordered to restore the widow's honour by marrying her, and was then executed, leaving his widow well provided for. Shakespeare would have found a version of this story in Giraldi Cinthio's collection, the *Hecatommithi* (1565), where he also found the story of the Moor and Disdemona that became *Othello*. In Cinthio's version, it is the brother of the heroine who is condemned, not her husband, and at the end she pleads for the life of the magistrate who has become her husband, and he is reprieved for a happy ending. Shakespeare also knew George Whetstone's play, *Promos and Cassandra* (1578), which adds a further complication: this time the condemned brother complains against the magistrate, and his life is secretly saved by his gaoler. When Cassandra pleads for the life of Promos in the play's final scene, it is the fact that her brother has not actually died that saves her husband's life. Whetstone also included a clumsy sub-plot of underworld characters that Shakespeare radically reworked.

When Shakespeare's heroine breaks the pattern of acquiescence, and rejects the magistrate's proposal, the tension rises and the whole direction of the story begins to change. Now the situation can only be resolved through the introduction of a new character, Mariana, who must be substituted for the heroine in the magistrate's bed, and it must be Mariana, rather than Isabella, who will plead for her husband's life, though as part of the play's theme of forgiveness she will be joined by Isabella, his intended victim. Shakespeare also used the bed-trick in *All's Well That Ends Well*, a play of uncertain date, though often assumed to have been written earlier than *Measure for Measure*. Both plays end with long and uncomfortable scenes in which the reluctant husbands, Bertram and Angelo, attempt to disclaim responsibility for their sexual acts and discredit their fiancées. For modern readers or audiences, the device of the bed-trick can seem stagey and artificial, yet *Measure for Measure* provides one of the more plausible examples of it. After all, Angelo has only seen Isabella twice, so that her visit in the dark, with only a single sentence spoken ('Remember now my brother'), easily allows another veiled woman to take her place.

The bed-trick is another folk motif, occurring in novella collections of the type Shakespeare often drew on for his plots, and after *All's Well* and *Measure for Measure* it began to be widely used in writing for the stage. Typically, bed-trick plots take one of two forms: in the first type of story, a bride is rejected by her groom unless she can meet a series of conditions – such as acquire her husband's ring, get a foal from his stallion, and become pregnant by him without his knowledge. When she meets these conditions, he embraces her and her children joyfully, and the conditions are seen as trials that she has successfully overcome. This is the outline of Boccaccio's tale of Giletta of Narbonne (the source for *All's Well That Ends Well*) in his *Decameron* (1349–51), later translated by William Painter in his *Palace of Pleasure* (1566–7, 1575). Painter also relates the story of 'The Two Gentlewomen of Venice' whose husbands desire each other's wives. The wives collude to prevent their husbands' infidelity by swapping beds with one another, so that each husband thinks he is having sex with his neighbour's wife, while he is actually with his own. Such containment of wandering desire within marriage usually results in the birth of sons, or even of twins because of the extra excitement it inspires, although wives quite naturally resent it. In both *All's Well* and *Measure for Measure*, an unwanted and unregarded fiancée rescues her (future) husband from the dangers of wandering desire. These plots allow 'both Bertram and Angelo to enact fantasies in which a virgin is soiled . . . only to find out that their sexual acts have in fact been legitimate, that the soiling has taken place only in fantasy. The bed-tricks thus offer to save Bertram and Angelo from their own fantasies' (Adelman, *Suffocating Mothers*, p. 77).

One prose fiction that Shakespeare knew well combined the story of a duke's retirement with that of a law against love (forbidding sex 'without solemnity of marriage'), a particularly elaborate example of the bed-trick, and a long final trial scene which explores the substantial gap between intentions and actions: this is Sir Philip Sidney's pastoral romance, the *Arcadia* (1590), which also supplied the sub-plot of *King Lear*. Duke Basileus and his wife Gynecia both make assignations to meet their lovers (as they suppose), in a dark cave where they actually encounter one another. The Duke, his imagination on fire, mistakes his wife for the Amazon Zelmane, while his wife realizes what has happened but cannot let on without compromising herself. Next morning, Basileus has nothing but praise for 'Zelmane', announcing with unconscious irony, 'O, who would have thought there could have been such difference betwixt women?' On hearing these words, his wife marvels at 'how much fancy doth not only darken reason but beguile our sense'. In the *Arcadia*, just as in *All's Well* and *Measure for*

Measure, the women realize what is going on, while the men are duped by the urgency of their desires, and in this respect – as in others – the bed-trick emphasizes the asymmetry of human biology, which requires male but not female arousal for the sexual act to take place (Shakespeare had already shown himself well aware of those implications in his poem *Venus and Adonis*).

The *Arcadia* ends with a lengthy trial scene in which the princes and the Duchess are accused of high treason and found guilty of killing Duke Basileus and conspiring to overthrow the state. While the reader knows that they had no such intentions, a series of accidents conspire to make it look as if that is what they had planned, and they are condemned to horrible deaths, but rescued in the nick of time when Duke Basileus unexpectedly recovers from a coma, mistaken for death. Their trial emphasizes the gap between intention and action, and the need to distinguish between them in the eyes of the law. In one particularly well-known Elizabethan law case (that of Hales versus Petit, 1562, probably referred to by the grave digger in *Hamlet*), the judge had stated that while there were three parts to any action – imagination, resolution and enactment – only the last could actually be taken into account. Edmund Plowden, the greatest jurist of the day, ruled that

For the imagination of the mind to do wrong, without an act done, is not punishable in our law, neither is the resolution to do that wrong, which he does not, punishable, but the doing of the act is the only point which the law regards; for until the act is done, it cannot be an offence to the world, and when the act is done, it is punishable. (*The Commentaries . . . of Edmund Plowden* (1816), Part I, p. 25)

The importance of 'enactment' in the eyes of the law will save Angelo from the consequences of what he had imagined and resolved to do.

MARRIAGE OR FORNICATION?

In the *Arcadia*, as in *Measure for Measure*, the law against lovers (or against sex outside marriage) carries the death penalty. Though there was no such law in Shakespeare's England, a few people argued that there should be, pointing out that it had existed in the Mosaic laws of the Old Testament, and had been seriously proposed by the Greek philosopher Plato in his book of *Laws*. To some radical Protestants, it seemed a possible solution to problems of sexual misbehaviour, and such a law was briefly introduced during the Commonwealth, though it did not survive long. In the play, it comes into direct conflict with the rather casual system of marriage that operated in Shakespeare's day. According to that system, a promise to marry made before witnesses (called a 'betrothal' or a 'hand-fasting') became legally binding if it was followed by sexual consummation – in effect, the promise being fulfilled. Marriages of this type were not at all popular with either the Church or the state, and in 1603 the Church made further efforts to stamp them out. Such marriages lacked 'the denunciation . . . of outward order', the calling of the banns, the public pledges made by the couple at the church door and the celebration of the mass. But though unpopular, they were undoubtedly legal and binding, so that, according to the English law of Shakespeare's day, both Claudio (knowingly) and Angelo (unknowingly) are not so much committing fornication as consummating their marriages, given that both have already made the necessary promises in advance before witnesses. Indeed, this is exactly the defence that Claudio offers when he is first arrested, explaining that it was

> upon a true contract
> I got possession of Julietta's bed.
> You know the lady. She is fast my wife
> Save that we do the denunciation lack
> Of outward order. (I.2.144–8)

The couple, like so many young couples in those days, were simply waiting for the release of the woman's dowry.

Angelo, too, had been pre-contracted to Mariana (as the disguised Duke somehow knows), but had broken off their engagement when her dowry, along with her brother, had been lost at sea. When he makes love to Mariana in the dark, in his garden house, it seems that his transgressive desires are being safely contained within marriage, against his conscious will and intention – rather as comparable desires had been in Painter's tale of 'The Two Gentlewomen of Venice' outlined above. As the judge appointed to Claudio's case, Angelo rejects his plea of good intent (though Escalus and the Provost are persuaded by it) and it is part of the complex 'Measure for Measure' justice that the play acts out, that by the end Angelo is forced to accept the mercy he does not want either to give or receive (in this, perhaps, resembling sinful mankind, confronted with Christ's merciful redemption?). Isabella's plea to the Duke for Angelo's life, made on behalf of Mariana (which recalls her plea to Angelo for her brother's life), turns on the legal distinction between action and intention, for she knows that Angelo has not succeeded in violating her, and has instead had sex with his (ex-) fiancée, a situation that Angelo had punished as fornication, when others had seen it as no more than an anticipation of marriage:

> My brother had but justice,
> In that he did the thing for which he died.
> For Angelo,
> His act did not o'ertake his bad intent,
> And must be buried but as an intent
> That perished by the way. Thoughts are no subjects,
> Intents but merely thoughts. (V.1.445–51)

The complex balance of 'Measure still for Measure' is maintained through the continuous paralleling of Claudio's case with Angelo's: Claudio is condemned to die but reprieved to marry (for all sorts of good, practical reasons), whereas Angelo is condemned to be married and then to die, but is also reprieved, to his apparent disappointment. As if Shakespeare is reappraising the tradition of marriage as the appropriate ending for a comedy, both Lucio and Angelo regard marriage as a punishment, while its significance for Isabella remains unknown because unspoken.

Isabella's words 'Thoughts are no subjects, | Intents but merely thoughts' define thoughts as lawless, insubordinate and potentially transgressive. Unlike bodies, which are subject to the state and its laws, thoughts are free. Thus, as Angelo's transgressive thoughts perform one action – the violation of Isabella – his dutiful body has been unknowingly (but not unwillingly) fulfilling his obligation to Mariana, and perhaps to the state. Thus two morally different actions are reconciled by the bed-trick, which allows him to imagine he is misbehaving, while saving him from the consequences of actually doing so. And the bed-trick poses a similarly complex question in terms of the greatest theological argument of Shakespeare's day. This turned upon how God's grace (expressed through the salvation of the soul after death) was to be achieved, though for most people 'Grace is grace, despite of all controversy', as Lucio observes at I.2.24–5. For Protestants, grace was acquired through faith, and for Catholics, through good works. This endlessly debated distinction is itself acted out in the bed-trick, since Angelo believes one thing while performing another. The act involves a loss of grace, as he later acknowledges ('Alack, when once our grace we have forgot, | Nothing goes right', IV.4.31–2), but it may also be redeemed through the intervention of Mariana, who converts Angelo's bad faith into an (involuntary and unconscious) good work by taking Isabella's place in his bed.

The gap identified by Isabella between thoughts and the body's subjection to the state acts as a reminder of the state's growing claims on the individual in early modern society, and the increasingly conflicting and conflicted nature of those claims. Nowhere did they operate more threateningly or more repressively than in the area of religion: individual resistance to state co-ercion was most passionate in the case of state-imposed religion. Censorship made it difficult for playwrights to represent this issue directly, but it would have been obvious to anyone who was a Roman Catholic (who had clung to the old religion), or a radical Protestant (who didn't think that the Protestant Reformation had gone far enough). The situation of a young woman under pressure to have sex with an authority figure, while innately dramatic, was particularly popular on the Elizabethan stage, and may well have symbolized the soul or spirit of the believer, oppressed by state machinery in a way that was widely recognized if never actually stated in so many words. It is, of course, the nub of *Measure for Measure*, where the heroine's initial desire to retreat to a convent is repeatedly interrupted and subverted. Fellow dramatists such as Thomas Dekker, Thomas Middleton, John Webster and Anthony Munday had employed this theme on behalf of their resisting Protestant heroines, and Shakespeare may simply have adopted their way of symbolizing the struggle between the individual and the state, or he may deliberately have written against that particular dramatic convention in presenting the plight of his Catholic heroine.

VIENNA OR LONDON?

The play's text, as printed in the First Folio, is exceptional in announcing its location at the outset – 'The scene Vienna'. But why did Shakespeare choose Vienna? Is it anything more than a light disguise for London? Vienna was one of the great capitals of the Holy Roman Empire, and 'the administrative hub of a vast and shifting Catholic alliance with which the English had been on hostile terms for decades' (Marcus, *Puzzling Shakespeare*, p. 162). Yet it was also peripheral and vulnerable, threatened by the expanding Turkish empire. In December 1604, King James's brother-in-law, the Duke of Holstein, was levying troops in London to lead into Hungary, where, two months earlier, a Protestant noble, Istvan Bocksai, had rebelled against the Empire and proclaimed himself king (and heir to the crown of St Stephen), with the aid of the Turks. The Duke of Holstein was going to his support, and this event may well lie behind the opening dialogue of Act I, scene 2:

LUCIO If the Duke, with the other dukes, come not to compo-
    sition with the King of Hungary, why then all the dukes
    fall upon the King.
FIRST GENTLEMAN Heaven grant us its peace, but not the
    King of Hungary's!
SECOND GENTLEMAN Amen.

Just as so many of the characters seem to have two
opposing facets, so does the play's location: Vienna can
be London, with its ruler sympathetically portrayed as a
version of James, striving to hold the balance between
different social elements and ultimately to behave gener-
ously to all of them; but if it is Vienna, it might have
been seen as a city of sleaze and corruption, where an
incompetent ruler has lost his grip and vice flourishes.
As Leah Marcus puts it, 'if Vienna is Vienna, or (worse
yet) a London *become* Vienna, then the play's topical
resonances turn completely inside out: all of the gestures
which seem to praise James in his triumphant mastery
over London can become elements in a dark fantasy of
alien Catholic domination' (*Puzzling Shakespeare*, p. 164).
Once Shakespeare had decided to make Isabella a
novice, and have the Duke disguise himself beneath a
friar's hood, the play needed to be set in a Catholic city,
for there had been neither nuns nor friars in England
since the Reformation had closed the monasteries and
convents more than half a century earlier. In any case,
unlike most of his contemporaries, Shakespeare did not
set his comedies in contemporary London but in unfa-
miliar, exotic settings – France, Italy, Athens, Illyria. Yet
the Duke's Vienna, and particularly its underworld characters, with their jokes and 'snatches' (IV.2.6), their
preoccupation with sex, drinking and eating, would have

seemed comfortably familiar to London theatregoers: 'Thus, what with the war, what with the sweat, what with the gallows, and what with poverty, I am custom-shrunk' (I.2.81–3), declares Mistress Overdone, the brothel madam, at her first entry, and though scholars now argue over the precise meaning of 'sweat' (a current epidemic? or the 'sweating tub' that was the only cure then available for venereal disease?), the first audiences would have known exactly what she was talking about.

London's theatres, including Shakespeare's Globe, stood outside the city walls in what were, technically speaking, the suburbs, surrounded by bear-baiting pits, alehouses, gambling dens and brothels. The theatre manager Philip Henslowe, who built the Rose theatre, the first theatre on Bankside, also owned the triple brothel, the Bell, Barge and Cock, next door to the Rose (though the major brothel owner on Bankside was the Bishop of Winchester!). The city authorities waged a continual battle with these overcrowded and disorderly areas that were technically outside their jurisdiction, and a major outbreak of the plague in 1603 provided a good excuse to close down the theatres and pull down the suburbs' slum housing. The city fathers (as they were called) were strongly Protestant, or puritan, and constituted a vocal group who took an active (or from another point of view, an interfering) part in the city's politics, and would have liked to see the theatres and brothels closed down in the name of good order, for their aim was to improve living conditions and thus transform society as a whole. A small minority of them even believed that fornication should be punishable by death (as it had been according to Old Testament law, which they took very seriously).

'Lord Angelo is precise', declares the Duke, where 'precise' can mean not only morally strict but also puritanical. 'Precision', a kind of spiritual fastidiousness, was a quality attributed to zealous puritans, and one that Angelo seems to display, making him a sort of tragic brother to Malvolio in *Twelfth Night* (for example, at II.4.9–15). Working towards a brave and virtuous new world, the city fathers found themselves clashing not only with the dissolute ways of the suburbs, but with the extravagant and theatrical style of the court in their midst, and it may be that, in the conflict between Angelo and the Duke, their measures and countermeasures register the ongoing struggle between more traditional systems of belief and social practice, and the reformers' desire to clean up and clear up murky areas of the law, for it was above all in the law courts that such conflicts were played out. English law, by the beginning of the seventeenth century, was a criss-cross of overlapping systems that included the canon law of the Church (now largely decided by the king and his government), the old common law of custom and established precedent (in need of clarification and codification) and the chancery law, the final court of appeal, which could override all the others; threading your way through these could be a complicated business.

Vienna's underworld is clearly in need of reform: beginning with the dialogue between Lucio and the two Gentlemen in the second scene of the play onwards, there are numerous nasty jokes about venereal disease and its effects – the resulting loss of hair or skin, blindness, bone-ache – and the sweating tubs that were the only available cure for syphilis, a repulsive, physically painful and highly infectious disease that was reaching epidemic proportions at the time this play was written. The dangers of too much sexual licence are darkly and unforgettably described by Claudio as he falls prey, not to infection, but to the new law:

> Our natures do pursue
> Like rats that ravin down their proper bane,
> A thirsty evil, and when we drink we die. (I.2.127–9)

But this vision of the self-destructive capacity of human beings, killing themselves in pursuit of sexual pleasure (one that can still be recognized today), is counterbalanced not merely by the public displays of forgiveness of the Duke and Isabella at the end of the play, but also by the steady decency of its minor officials – the kindliness and concern of the Provost, and the patience of Escalus in Act II, scene 1, where he tries to establish what it was that Froth actually did to Elbow's wife when she came in with a longing for stewed prunes, in the face of Elbow's misuse of words and Pompey's attempts to deflect or distort the constable's accusations. Escalus dismisses Pompey and Froth with a caution, and shows some concern for Elbow's feelings, while trying to find a replacement for him. On hearing how long Elbow has served, Escalus replies, 'Alas, it hath been great pains to you; they do you wrong to put you so oft upon't. Are there not men in your ward sufficient to serve it?' (II.1.253–5). The conduct of this particular Viennese magistrate suggests ways in which English justices of the peace might temper government initiatives to the needs of their particular communities. His genuine and practical human kindness is heartening, as well as reassuring: 'So shines a good deed in a naughty world' (*Merchant of Venice*, V.1.91).

One final image of the play's multiple meanings – this time an offstage image that must be imagined by the audience – is one with a wide, and widely conflicting range of referents. It stands at the heart of the play's accumulating sexual fantasies, a vision of a paradise lost through the degraded desires of the city and, in particular, of Shakespeare's London, where, according to the puritan critic Philip Stubbes, 'In the fields and suburbs of the cities they have gardens, either paled, or walled round about very high, with their arbours and bowers fit for the purpose' (*Anatomy of Abuses* (1583), p. 88). Isabella reports to Mariana and the disguised Duke that Angelo

> hath a garden circummured with brick,
> Whose western side is with a vineyard backed;
> And to that vineyard is a planchèd gate,
> That makes his opening with this bigger key.
> This other doth command a little door
> Which from the vineyard to the garden leads.
> There have I made my promise,
> Upon the heavy middle of the night,
> To call upon him. (IV.1.27–35)

The fact that 'he did show me | The way twice o'er' (39–40) reveals Angelo's eagerness, anxiety, obsession and attention to detail. The privacy of the walled garden that opens with a little key is among the oldest images for a woman's body as an object of desire – as such it had been used as a literary image for sexual pleasure and possession at least since the biblical Song of Solomon. But the garden with its outer wall, its 'planchèd gate' (like modern garden doors) opening into the vineyard, and the smaller key for the door that opens the inner garden also reflects the play's several retreats from public to private worlds, from the freedom of the streets to the secrecy of the garden. Its little world of walls within walls recalls the play's other enclosed locations: the walled city of Vienna surrounds the walled prison, and the convent of the poor Clares where Isabella hopes to find 'more strict restraint' (I.4.4), as well as Mariana's 'moated grange' (III.1.265). *Measure for Measure* dramatizes the struggle between the desire for confinement – within the rules of the state, or the religious life, or marriage – and the desire for freedom, with all the risks that 'too much liberty' (I.2.124) may bring. Such conflicting impulses are still at work today, not only in our private lives, but also on the political stage, where they operate as powerfully as they did four hundred years ago.

Julia Briggs

The Play in Performance

On stage, *Measure for Measure* is an exciting play to watch. From the Duke's obscure and difficult opening speech, the action rushes on headlong, pausing only briefly over Elbow's lexical confusions, Isabella and Angelo's tormented soliloquies and the mournful ditty sung at Mariana's moated grange, 'Take, O take those lips away' (IV.1). Even an inept director would find it difficult to make this play boring, consisting, as it does, in a series of dramatic confrontations, in which largely well-intentioned characters attempt to persuade or coerce, bully and even blackmail one another into various actions, for various ends. The climax is a long final scene of almost classical reversals and recognitions, revelations and exposures, in which muffled-up mysteries are made plain and 'Pardon's the word to all' (*Cymbeline*, V.5.422).

Although the play thus to some extent dictates its own rhythms, there have been widely differing critical interpretations of its main characters over the last half-century, as changing attitudes to political authority, to sexual hypocrisy and female chastity have affected both reception and performance, and the advent of feminism, in particular, has changed our response to Isabella's oppression and her desire for self-determination. The portrayal of the Duke has varied greatly: in earlier centuries, the

traditional stage hero who saved the day; more recently
he has come to be seen as a saint, a compulsive meddler,
a portrait of King James I, a political gangster and even
a mini-dictator. Freudian theory has cast new light on
the repressed Angelo, making him less of a fallen angel
and more of a suitable case for treatment, as the helpless
victim of his own compulsions. In performance, the play
inevitably turns on how the roles of Isabella, Angelo and
the Duke are interpreted, but minor characters, or those
who have little to say, can make a bigger impact on the
stage than on the page. This is most obviously true of
the comic roles (at the end of the eighteenth and the
beginning of the nineteenth century, popular comedians
'Dicky' Suett and John Liston famously played Pompey).
But it also applies to the Provost, a near-silent presence
in a surprisingly large number of scenes, and to the pregnant Juliet. Though she is given very few lines, her mere
appearance serves as a reminder of rebirth and natural
growth, of the 'teeming foison' (I.4.43) of the green
world beyond the play's looming deaths and executions
– the world of Shakespeare's earlier comedies.

   The most influential production in the twentieth
century revitalized critical and theatrical interest and for
many years was regarded as the definitive version: this
was Peter Brook's production at Stratford in 1950, with
a star-studded cast that included John Gielgud as Angelo,
Harry Andrews as the Duke, and the nineteen-year-old
Barbara Jefford as Isabella; in the smaller roles Alan
Badel played Claudio and Robert Hardy and Robert Shaw
had walk-on parts as the First and Second Gentleman.
Brook's production was influenced by, while reacting
against, that of Tyrone Guthrie at the Old Vic in 1933.
Here, Charles Laughton had played Angelo as 'a cunning
oleaginous monster, whose cruelty and lubricity could

have surprised no one, least of all himself' (Guthrie, *A Life in the Theatre* (1960), p. 110), with Flora Robson as Isabella, and a young James Mason as Claudio.

Characterizing his sense of the play in *The Empty Space*, Brook saw it as dominated by two conflicting moods which he designated 'Holy' and 'Rough' theatre:

the disgusting, stinking world of medieval Vienna . . . is absolutely necessary to the meaning of the play: Isabella's plea for grace has far more meaning in this Dostoevskian setting than it would in lyrical comedy's never-never land . . . it demands an absolutely convincing roughness and dirt. Also, when so much of the play is religious in thought, the loud humour of the brothel is important as a device, because it is alienating and humanising. (1990, p. 99)

Angus McBean's photographs of Brook's production convey its powerful visual impact, set beneath a sequence of arches that stood for the play's several enclosures: as the walls of Vienna, they revealed an open sky beyond, or else overshadowed a prison filled with instruments of torture. The actors' costumes and the curiously curved pikes carried by the guards recalled Brueghel's painting of invading Spanish soldiers, 'Massacre of Innocents' (*c.* 1565). The Duke was played firmly within the critical tradition established by G. Wilson Knight in 1930, as a wise and holy man, while Angelo was a tragic figure, who could not keep his hands off Isabella, yet was horrified and heart-broken at what he was doing. Isabella pleaded with youthful passion for her brother, and everyone who saw it remembered the sustained pause after Mariana's line at V.1.439, 'O Isabel, will you not lend a knee?' Brook famously instructed Barbara Jefford to hold the pause 'until she felt the audience could take

it no longer' (p. 100). This moment opened up the possibility that, on stage at least, and particularly in the final
scene, what Isabella doesn't say is quite as important as
what she does, and since then, the play's 'open silences'
have attracted the interest of both directors and critics,
though of course they can only be inferred from the text,
being, by definition, absent or silent.

The greatest of the text's silences occurs in response
to the Duke's two proposals to Isabella, at V.i.489 and
534. While her acceptance was probably a foregone
conclusion for Shakespeare's audience, it looks rather
different today, though Brook's Isabella had no difficulty
in accepting his wise and manly Duke. Although this
production was felt in its time to be highly convincing,
Brook had in fact introduced a very different kind of
silence, at points where the play-text speaks, by making
a number of strategic cuts. In doing so he was following
an old-fashioned theatrical tradition according to which
this (not very long) play was substantially cut in performance. Brook omitted most of Lucio's criticisms of the
Duke in order to achieve a cleaner and less complicated
story-line than Shakespeare had provided, and he reduced
the low-life scenes, as if worried that they might hold up
the action (as they are surely intended to do).

Despite his cavalier treatment of the text, Brook's
production rediscovered the play for the stage, and there-
after it acquired a popularity never previously achieved.
Surviving records of its earliest stage history are sporadic:
after that first note of its performance at court on 26
December 1604, no further performances are recorded
until 1662 when William Davenant put on a Restoration
version crossed with *Much Ado About Nothing*, which he
entitled *The Law Against Lovers* (Angelo was identified
with the then discredited Lord Protector, Oliver

Cromwell). In 1699, Charles Gildon rewrote the play again (as *Measure for Measure, or Beauty the Best Advocate*), this time combining it with Henry Purcell's opera *Dido and Aeneas*, but by 1720 a more authentic version had reached the stage, with David Garrick's rival James Quin playing the Duke (then and later regarded as the starring role, rather than that of Angelo). Towards the end of the century, John Philip Kemble, an actor in the Quin tradition, took over the part and published an acting version that ironed out the play's sudden switches of mood, scene and atmosphere, as well as its explicit allusions to sexuality.

Kemble's sister, Mrs Siddons, the greatest Shakespearian actress of her day, starred opposite him as Isabella, a role she had first played at Drury Lane in 1783. Although Claudio refers explicitly to his sister's youth (at I.2.181), Mrs Siddons continued to play Isabella for the next thirty years, until she could not get up off her knees after the Duke's proposal without a helping hand. Individual actresses have been criticized as being too old for Isabella: Margaret Johnston was 'too much the shrewish, maiden-auntish defender of her chastity' in 1956 (Kenneth Young, quoted in Gay, *As She Likes It*, p. 126), or else too young – Judi Dench, making her Stratford debut in 1962, was too 'kittenish'. The relative ages of the main characters can become a crucial issue in performance, the age of the Duke in particular making him seem either a more or a less suitable match for Isabella.

Measure for Measure appealed strongly to several great romantic writers, including Pushkin, and Richard Wagner created a proto-feminist adaptation of it as the libretto for his early opera, *Das Liebesverbot* ('Love Forbidden', 1836). He omitted the Duke entirely, kept the pregnant

Juliet offstage and left all the plotting in the hands of a capable Isabella. She leads the people of Palermo (its new and suitably Italianate setting) in a revolt, rescuing Claudio from prison along the way. At the end, she claims the hand of her brother's best friend, Lucio, who has secretly loved her all along. The underworld subplot is transformed into a *commedia dell'arte* entertainment.

Nearer home, *Measure for Measure* remained comparatively neglected through the nineteenth century because of its 'indelicate' subject-matter (the version rewritten for children by Charles and Mary Lamb was scarcely comprehensible). The most influential production was that of Samuel Phelps in 1846, in which he played the Duke (it probably prompted Holman Hunt's painting of Isabella and Claudio in the prison). In an age of Shakespeare spectaculars, Phelps restored lines that had traditionally been cut and scenes that had been altered, and he simplified scenery and effects, creating a more rapid and continuous action on stage. His practice was to influence that of William Poel and Harley Granville-Barker, early in the following century.

Poel opened his revolutionary season at the Royalty Theatre in 1893 with *Measure for Measure*, played in Elizabethan costume on a reconstructed Elizabethan stage. Here, and later, Poel attempted to reproduce what he knew of the original stage conditions, and his style influenced performances during the twenties. Until Poel, the play was normally staged in vaguely medieval costume, with Isabella as a wimpled nun. Guthrie and Brook maintained this tradition, though Jefford's Isabella did not wear a nun's habit but a sober dress with a shawl over her hair. In the second half of the twentieth century, however, the play came to seem more contemporary. For Jonathan Miller in 1974, Freud's Vienna was the obvious location for a play so centrally concerned with the effects of sexual pathology. Since then, a number of productions have adopted modern dress, setting the play in an unidentified fascist regime, as did Nicholas Hytner with the Royal Shakespeare Company in 1987, or else in the bleak post-war Vienna of Carol Reed's film, *The Third Man* (1949). In Michael Boyd's production at the RSC in 1998, the relationship between public and private conduct was felt to be crucial, and the Duke delivered his opening speech on a gramophone record (as in Hytner's 1987 production), while at the National Theatre in 2004 Simon McBurney's production for Complicité carefully distinguished between public and private words through the use of microphones and video-cameras.

John Barton's production at Stratford in 1970 marked another turning point in the play's history, when his Isabella, Estelle Kohler, rejected the Duke's proposal in the final scene. She turned away from him and remained alone on stage at the end, looking at the audience as if uncertain what to do next. Suddenly critics who had previously found Isabella selfish, prim or prudish, began to see the point: 'Why should she surrender her body, as if it were trivial, to save one man from another's punishment?' In Barton's version, the Duke, played by Sebastian Shaw, was 'a late middle-aged, bookish, bumbling ruler, saddened but not surprised when Isabella reacted with utter dismay to his proposal' (Gay, p. 129). His age made him seem an impossible match to Isabella's eyes.

The possibility that Isabella might reject the Duke, as she had done in Barton's production, led in turn to a sense that if she was going to accept him, her response should be something more than a matter of submission and compliance, especially since Isabella has already shown herself unusually resistant to submission and compliance. The solution adopted was one that had recently become popular in productions of *The Taming of the Shrew* (in the wake of the Burton and Taylor film of 1967): to have Isabella and the Duke fall in love long before the final scene, although nothing in the text justifies such an interpretation. Thus Barry Kyle's production for the RSC in 1978 had Michael Pennington playing the Duke as the romantic lead, 'young and good-looking, mischievous and generous'. Paola Dionisotti's Isabella joined in his schemes with alacrity, and there was 'a good deal of chummy kissing and hugging between them' (Gay, p. 134), while Jonathan Pryce as Angelo was correspondingly diminished to 'a neurotic little civil servant, always twitchy and awkward' (Helen Reid, quoted in Gay, p. 134). Adrian Noble's 1983 production, lavishly set in late eighteenth-century Italy, also focused upon the unfolding relationship between Daniel Massey's serious and spiritual Duke and Juliet Stevenson's uniquely passionate and intelligent Isabella – a relationship in which she responded to his tests with creative solutions that seemed to promise something more than the usual storybook ending. With Stevenson's emancipated and self-knowing Isabella (she scarcely paused over Mariana's request in the final scene, but immediately knelt beside her in sisterly solidarity), 'late twentieth-century feminism' (Gay, p. 139) had 'come of age'.

A strong Duke can often have the effect of diminishing the role of Angelo, and vice versa. Brook's production was particularly lucky in being able to balance the Angelo of John Gielgud (the greatest Shakespearian actor of the twentieth century) against the charismatic Duke of Harry Andrews, but Ian Richardson's sinister Angelo in John Barton's 1970 version was contrasted with Sebastian Shaw's ineffectual and bespectacled Duke. The play was filmed for television in 1979, as part of the BBC/Time-Life series, and in this version a powerful and ruthless Angelo, played by the compulsively watchable Tim Pigott-Smith (soon to star as a sadistic British officer in *The Jewel in the Crown*) challenged a strong Isabella in Kate Nelligan, but left the Duke searching for his role in the play. This was one of the earliest films to be made in the BBC's five-year project, and the director, Desmond Davis, concentrated on the visual dimension, dressing his characters in sombre Jacobean costume and setting his scenes among sunlit neoclassical courtyards and in a prison of deep shadows that recalled Rembrandt's engravings. One reviewer, H. R. Coursen, noticed that the play

seems almost to have been written for television. Not only is it melodramatic and episodic, but, as episodic narratives often are, it is a series of vivid one-on-one confrontations. Such scenes work very well within the limited space of (a) a studio, and (b) a picture tube. (*Shakespeare and the Moving Image*, p. 12)

As Angelo, Tim Pigott-Smith was confidently hypocritical: his 'Who will believe thee, Isabel?' (II.4.154, with its insolently intimate form of address) was thrown out with calm and contempt. On the other hand, the Duke (Kenneth Colley), having once surrendered his authority, never appeared to recapture it. He seemed abstracted or absent-minded, marooned between a high-principled Isabella and the sheer psychic weight of Angelo. A sense that the Duke might be quite as uncertain of himself as his critics were was further developed in Nicholas Hytner's 1987 production for Stratford, where Sean Baker's rapacious Angelo was offset by a Duke (played by Roger Allam) who seemed absorbed in solving the enigma of his own personality, chronically incapable of making up his mind, puzzled as to where he was going or what he should do next. This was a new and unexpected interpretation, though after the opening scene, it strained somewhat against the grain of the text. Yet an uncertain Duke (such as Kenneth Colley and Roger Allam played) is at least seriously engaged with the character's inconsistencies as recorded in the text: Allam seemed to feel his way into the Duke's lines and his elusive personality.

A rather different take on the ambiguous Duke featured in Simon McBurney's 2004 production for the National: David Troughton, looking plump and avuncular, seemed at first shy and well intentioned, but when he finally proposed to Isabella, the audience heard the (by then familiar) clang of the prison door, and saw, lit up at the back of the stage, the marriage bed which now seemed only a long-drawn-out version of the execution block. We recalled that Angelo and Lucio had already begged for death in preference to marriage.

But the threat of marriage to the Duke, gruesome though it might be, paled in this production beside Angelo's onstage abuse of Isabella in their second confrontation in Act II, scene 4, where Paul Rhys as Angelo pulled Isabella's hand inside his trousers, while Naomi Frederick's face silently registered her horror, disgust and helplessness. By the time she had reached 'To whom should I complain?' (171), she was practically choking. Ian Richardson, the notably sinister Angelo in John Barton's 1970 production more than thirty years earlier, recalled that censorship had been withdrawn two months after the play had opened. In consultation with Isabella (Estelle Kohler), he reworked the staging of that particular scene, so that 'I physically abused her and pressed my hands firmly up her skirts. I also felt that Angelo's sexuality was rather sinister, so I asked Estelle if we could do some business where I pulled her hair' (Gay, p. 131).

Actually Peter Brook's 1950 production had already introduced a degree of physical violence into this scene, as the surviving prompt book indicates: 'Angelo grasps her arms, holds her against table', 'Angelo cross to Isab[ella], grasps her wrists, slams door'. As we have seen, subsequent productions have taken Angelo's brutality several steps further. In Nicholas Hytner's 1987 production, Sean Baker's Angelo knocked Josette Simon's Isabella to the floor at 'Who will believe thee, Isabel?' (II.4.154) and all but raped her. In 1992, the Compass Theatre Company performed a version of *Measure for Measure* at Buxton with a tiny cast and a great deal of doubling, in which Isabella and Mistress Overdone were played by the same actress; Angelo, Claudio and Barnadine were played by the same actor, and the Duke and Elbow doubled as the play's (incompetent) authority figures. According to Michael Hattaway, the effect of linking Angelo and Claudio together so closely was to lay bare the play's misogyny (*Shakespeare Survey 46*).

The Compass Theatre Company was probably influenced by an even more radical adaptation made by Charles Marowitz for the Open Space in 1975, which omitted Mariana, the Duke's disguise and the bed-trick, and redistributed many of the play's lines so that they acquired a sardonic or cynical twist. In this version, both the Duke and a new character, 'the Bishop', condone Angelo's misbehaviour, and join him to make up a smug and rapacious all-male gang who have got the city's action well wrapped up. This version was inspired, as Marowitz explained, by his experience of having been mistakenly arrested for shoplifting and vagrancy. His treatment as a non-person made him realize what he had in common with Isabella, in the play. Revised for performance in Los Angeles, his version ends with a nightmare in which Isabella is hunted down by the play's various male characters:

In the final scene, having been stirred by Isabella's vulnerability, more so than by her suit, [the Duke] coolly decides to appropriate her for himself. (Having been 'had' by Angelo, she is already, in his eyes, damaged goods.) As she flees from his embrace, her exit is barred by Angelo. As she tries to escape in the other direction, she is intercepted by a predatory Lucio. As she tries to avoid him, she runs smack into a reincarnated Claudio, in whose eyes she reads the same lustful intent that she found in the other men. As the regent, the deputy, the rake and the executed fornicator back her into a corner and simultaneously bear down on her, the lights mercifully fade. (Marowitz, p. 48)

Isabella's sexual exploitation, the oppression of an individual by the machinery of the state, is what gives the play its political immediacy, and her torment and helplessness are just as painful, whether we picture her as suffering under the oppression of the religious state that, in Shakespeare's lifetime, pursued, tortured and executed extreme Protestants and Catholics, or whether we see her as the victim of the modern secular state, which has similarly persecuted political, sexual and ethnic outsiders, whether communists, homosexuals, Jews, Muslims or any other distinctive social group. The corruption of authority and the victimization of the individual seem to be unavoidable features of human systems of government and law – tragic truths, from which Shakespeare wrests this uneasy, thought-provoking comedy.

Julia Briggs

Further Reading

There are three excellent editions of *Measure for Measure* on a more ambitious scale than the present one, providing more detailed glosses and commentary and further information about the play's sources, dating and themes; the two more recent also give short performance histories. Though J. W. Lever's edition for Arden 2nd series (1965) is the earliest, its thoughtful analysis and fine judgement make it well worth consulting half a century later. Brian Gibbons's edition for Cambridge University Press (1991) and N. W. Bawcutt's for Oxford University Press (1991) establish helpful historical contexts (in significantly different ways), and both pay attention to the play's various textual problems (the sole surviving text is that of the First Folio). Mark Eccles has edited the New Variorum Shakespeare edition (1980) which includes much material from earlier critics and editions, and Ernst Leisi's 'Old-Spelling and Old-Meaning Edition' of the play (1964) focuses, as its title implies, on language and meaning.

The one-volume Oxford Shakespeare, edited by Stanley Wells and Gary Taylor, proposes that *Measure for Measure* (here edited by John Jowett) was significantly revised by Thomas Middleton in the early 1620s, and that his revision explains some of the textual anomalies. Their case is set out in full in John Jowett and Gary Taylor's *Shakespeare Reshaped, 1606–23* (1993) and deserves to be taken into account. Gary Taylor's forthcoming *Complete Works of Thomas Middleton* will highlight the passages attributed to Middleton. There is a collection of essays on the play by C. K. Stead in the Casebook Series (1971) and a more recent volume of *Critical Essays* edited by Richard P. Wheeler (1999).

To a large extent, the history of the play's critical reputation and its performance history go hand in hand. Charlotte Lennox, writing in the mid-eighteenth century, thought Shakespeare had 'made a wrong choice of his subject' in the play, and that the story was unsuitable for comedy, while Coleridge considered it 'the single exception to the delightfulness of Shakespeare's plays', disturbing and distasteful. European romantic critics such as Schlegel, less troubled by the subject, were more appreciative. English sexual taboos made the play something of an embarrassment during the nineteenth century. In the last chapter of *The Genius of Shakespeare* (1997), Jonathan Bate starts with Thomas Bowdler and his difficulties with *Measure for Measure* and goes on to use the play's critical history as a way of outlining twentieth-century responses to Shakespeare more generally. Invoking the concepts of relativity and uncertainty from modern physics, he stages a debate between the old-fashioned certainties of 'Q' (Sir Arthur Quiller-Couch) in his 1922 introduction to the New Shakespeare edition of the play, contrasting it with William Empson's concept of ambiguity. Empson examined the phrase 'their proper bane' (I.2.128) as an example of the fifth of his *Seven Types of Ambiguity* (1930).

The play re-established itself both critically and in performance at the beginning of the 1920s – as Rosalind

Miles recorded in *The Problem of 'Measure for Measure'* (1976) and more recently T. F. Wharton in his account of the play for The Critics Debate series (1989). While often invoking the problem of Isabella's character, mid-twentieth-century criticism has more often turned on the nature of the Duke and his authority – G. Wilson Knight's chapter on '*Measure for Measure* and the Gospels', in *The Wheel of Fire* (1930), set the agenda. In it, he interpreted the play in the light of the Sermon on the Mount and the parables of the New Testament, representing the Duke as a Christ-like figure of forgiveness. F. R. Leavis's essay on the play in *The Common Pursuit* (1952) defended Knight's position, but it came under heavy attack from later critics. There were adverse responses from Clifford Leech in 'The "Meaning" of *Measure for Measure*', *Shakespeare Survey 3* (1950); from William Empson in '*Sense* in *Measure for Measure*', in *The Structure of Complex Words* (1951); from A. P. Rossiter in *Angel with Horns* (1961); from A. D. Nuttall in '*Measure for Measure*: Quid Pro Quo?', *Shakespeare Studies 4* (1968); and from Graham Bradshaw in 'On Tempering Mercy with Justice' in *Shakespeare's Scepticism* (1987). The Duke's virtue was scrutinized from a range of different positions, using a variety of arguments. More recently, Harry Berger Jr, in *Making Trifles of Terror* (1997), returned to the problems posed by the Duke to ask a series of searching questions about what exactly happens in the final minutes of the play – questions that invite critical speculation, though in performance they require definite answers. Lars Engle finds one in the awkward combination of authority and scepticism that the Duke displays – see his '*Measure for Measure*: The Sceptic's Authority', in *Shakespeare and Modernity*, ed. Hugh Grady (2000). An altogether different solution was proposed as early as 1931, when W. W. Lawrence argued that Vincentio was less a human being than a theatrical device, 'a stage Duke, and not a real person', in *Shakespeare's Problem Comedies*. Anne Barton, in *Shakespeare and the Idea of the Play* (1962), took the idea of the Duke's theatricality a step further, suggesting that in some sense he was the playwright at work within the play.

From the 1970s, feminist criticism has resulted in new readings of the play. Janet Adelman offers a particularly interesting analysis of 'the fundamental incompatibility between marriage and male desire' in chapter 4 of her book *Suffocating Mothers* (1992). Other critics have adopted even gloomier positions. Kate McLuskie, in her essay 'The Patriarchal Bard', in *Political Shakespeare*, ed. Jonathan Dollimore and Alan Sinfield (1985), argued that 'Feminist criticism of this play is restricted to exposing its own exclusion from the text. It has no point of entry.' Jacqueline Rose's essay on 'Sexuality in the reading of Shakespeare', in *Alternative Shakespeares*, ed. John Drakakis (1985), provides a psychoanalytical reading of the play's complex interaction between male fantasy, language and subjectivity. Harriett Hawkins's Introduction to *Measure for Measure*, on the other hand, celebrates the play's arguments and contradictions with characteristic good humour and common sense (1987). Kate Chedgzoy's study of it in the series Writers and their Work (2000) also serves as a helpful introduction, concentrating particularly on how gender operates in performance.

Geoffrey Bullough's *Narrative and Dramatic Sources*, vol. II: *Comedies* (1958) provides texts of the play's main antecedents (including the story from St Augustine). Leah Scragg gives an interesting account of the plot and the folktale elements in *Shakespeare's Alternative Tales* (1996).

For the significance of the bed-trick, the mechanism on which the plot turns, see A. D. Nuttall's article '*Measure for Measure*: The Bed-Trick', *Shakespeare Survey 28* (1975), and my own article on 'Shakespeare's Bed-Tricks', in *Essays in Criticism* 44, no. 4 (1994); Marliss C. Desens's study, *The Bed-Trick in English Renaissance Drama* (1994), offers a wider perspective.

One of the earliest and still one of the best of historicist accounts is Elizabeth M. Pope's 'The Renaissance Background to *Measure for Measure*', *Shakespeare Survey 2* (1949) – it is especially informative on the significance of the play's theology. On the play's first performance, see Josephine Waters Bennett, *'Measure for Measure' as Royal Entertainment* (1966), and on its religious, legal and moral arguments, Darryl J. Gless in *'Measure for Measure': The Law and the Convent* (1979). Debora Shuger's *Political Theologies in Shakespeare's England* (2001) explores the close connections between theology and politics in early modern thought, deploying some less familiar material in the course of a series of controversial arguments.

Inevitably, given their concern with the impact of power on cultural production, New Historicists have found the play particularly relevant to their concerns. Stephen Greenblatt's essay 'Martial Law in the Land of Cockaigne', in *Shakespearean Negotiations* (1988), explores the use of anxiety as a means of social control, while noting the Duke's ineffective attempts to exercise such control. Jonathan Dollimore in 'Transgression and Surveillance in *Measure for Measure*' (in *Political Shakespeare*, as above) redefines the play's conflict between authority and sexual transgression to show that the state asserts its authority by actively repressing and making scapegoats of sexual offenders. Leonard

Tennenhouse's essay 'Representing Power: *Measure for Measure* in its Time', in *The Power of Forms in the English Renaissance*, ed. Stephen Greenblatt (1982), considers the play as one of several 'disguised ruler' plays that aimed to restore the monarch 'to a natural position of supremacy as a father over a family'. Jonathan Goldberg's account of the play in his book *James I and the Politics of Literature* (1983) argues that 'the essential question that links politics and literature in the Jacobean period is representation', reading the play as an analysis of representation, as practised both by the king and by the dramatist himself. Leah Marcus explores the play's London connections in her rich chapter on it in *Puzzling Shakespeare* (1988). For more on the playhouses and the suburbs, see Stephen Mullaney, *The Place of the Stage* (1988), and on London more generally, Lawrence Manley's anthology *London in the Age of Shakespeare* (1986). Jean Howard, in her essay 'Shakespeare and Genre', in *A Companion to Shakespeare*, ed. David Scott Kastan (1999), argues that the play should be read in the context of other city comedies.

As well as histories of the play in performance in the Oxford and Cambridge editions, there is a volume on *Measure for Measure* in the Text and Performance series by Graham Nicholls (1986). The annual *Shakespeare Survey* carries reviews of performances and these can be supplemented by more focused explorations such as Penny Gay's *As She Likes It: Shakespeare's Unruly Women* (1994) and Carol Chillington Rutter's *Clamorous Voices: Shakespeare's Women Today* (1988). Peter Brook recorded the aims of his 1950 production in *The Empty Space* (1968; Penguin, 1990) and Herbert S. Weil Jr exposed its silent cuts in 'The options of the audience: theory and practice in Peter Brook's *Measure for Measure*', *Shakespeare Survey 28* (1975). The 'open silences' of the

ending were first explored by Philip C. McGuire in
Speechless Dialect: Shakespeare's Open Silences (1985) and
reconsidered by Edward L. Rocklin in 'Measured
Endings: how productions from 1720 to 1929 close
Shakespeare's open silences in *Measure for Measure*',
Shakespeare Survey 52 (2000). H. R. Coursen's response
to the BBC TV film of *Measure for Measure* is quoted
from *Shakespeare and the Moving Image*, ed. Anthony
Davies and Stanley Wells (1994), and the account of the
Compass Theatre production at Bradford in 1992 is from
Michael Hattaway's essay on 'Male Sexuality and
Misogyny', *Shakespeare Survey* 46 (1994), reprinted in
Shakespeare and Sexuality, ed. C. Alexander and S. Wells
(2001). Charles Marowitz's version of *Measure for
Measure* and the Los Angeles addition can be found in
his *Recycling Shakespeare* (1991).

Julia Briggs

MEASURE FOR MEASURE

The Characters in the Play

Vincentio, the DUKE
ANGELO, the Deputy
ESCALUS, an ancient Lord
CLAUDIO, a young Gentleman
LUCIO, a Fantastic
Two other like GENTLEMEN
PROVOST
FRIAR THOMAS
FRIAR PETER
ELBOW, a simple Constable
FROTH, a foolish Gentleman
POMPEY, a Clown, servant to Mistress Overdone
ABHORSON, an Executioner
BARNARDINE, a dissolute Prisoner
JUSTICE
Varrius, a friend to the Duke
ISABELLA, a sister to Claudio
MARIANA, betrothed to Angelo
JULIET, beloved of Claudio
FRANCISCA, a Nun
MISTRESS OVERDONE, a Bawd

Lords and Attendants
Officers

Citizens
SERVANTS
A BOY
A MESSENGER

The scene Vienna
Enter Duke, Escalus, Lords, and Attendants

DUKE

Escalus.

ESCALUS

My lord.

DUKE

Of government the properties to unfold
Would seem in me t'affect speech and discourse,
Since I am put to know that your own science
Exceeds, in that, the lists of all advice
My strength can give you. Then no more remains
But that, to your sufficiency, as your worth is able,
And let them work. The nature of our people,
Our city's institutions, and the terms   10
For common justice, y'are as pregnant in
As art and practice hath enrichèd any
That we remember. There is our commission,
From which we would not have you warp. Call hither,
I say, bid come before us Angelo.   *Exit an Attendant*
What figure of us think you he will bear?
For you must know, we have with special soul
Elected him our absence to supply,
Lent him our terror, dressed him with our love,

20   And given his deputation all the organs
      Of our own power. What think you of it?
ESCALUS
      If any in Vienna be of worth
      To undergo such ample grace and honour,
      It is Lord Angelo.

      Enter Angelo

DUKE   Look where he comes.

ANGELO
      Always obedient to your grace's will,
      I come to know your pleasure.

DUKE   Angelo,
      There is a kind of character in thy life
      That to th'observer doth thy history
      Fully unfold. Thyself and thy belongings
30   Are not thine own so proper as to waste
      Thyself upon thy virtues, they on thee.
      Heaven doth with us as we with torches do,
      Not light them for themselves: for if our virtues
      Did not go forth of us, 'twere all alike
      As if we had them not. Spirits are not finely touched
      But to fine issues, nor Nature never lends
      The smallest scruple of her excellence
      But, like a thrifty goddess, she determines
      Herself the glory of a creditor,
40   Both thanks and use. But I do bend my speech
      To one that can my part in him advertise.
      Hold therefore, Angelo:
      In our remove be thou at full ourself.
      Mortality and mercy in Vienna
      Live in thy tongue and heart. Old Escalus,
      Though first in question, is thy secondary.
      Take thy commission.

ANGELO   Now, good my lord,

Let there be some more test made of my metal
Before so noble and so great a figure
Be stamped upon it.

DUKE   No more evasion.   50
We have with a leavened and preparèd choice
Proceeded to you; therefore take your honours.
Our haste from hence is of so quick condition
That it prefers itself, and leaves unquestioned
Matters of needful value. We shall write to you,
As time and our concernings shall importune,
How it goes with us, and do look to know
What doth befall you here. So fare you well.
To th'hopeful execution do I leave you
Of your commissions.

ANGELO   Yet give leave, my lord,   60
That we may bring you something on the way.

DUKE
My haste may not admit it;
Nor need you, on mine honour, have to do
With any scruple. Your scope is as mine own,
So to enforce or qualify the laws
As to your soul seems good. Give me your hand.
I'll privily away: I love the people,
But do not like to stage me to their eyes;
Though it do well, I do not relish well
Their loud applause and aves vehement,   70
Nor do I think the man of safe discretion
That does affect it. Once more, fare you well.

ANGELO
The heavens give safety to your purposes!

ESCALUS
Lead forth and bring you back in happiness!

DUKE
I thank you. Fare you well.   *Exit*

ESCALUS

    I shall desire you, sir, to give me leave
    To have free speech with you, and it concerns me
    To look into the bottom of my place.
    A power I have, but of what strength and nature
80   I am not yet instructed.

ANGELO

    'Tis so with me. Let us withdraw together,
    And we may soon our satisfaction have
    Touching that point.

ESCALUS   I'll wait upon your honour. *Exeunt*

I.2   *Enter Lucio and two other Gentlemen*

LUCIO If the Duke, with the other dukes, come not to
    composition with the King of Hungary, why then all the
    dukes fall upon the King.

FIRST GENTLEMAN Heaven grant us its peace, but not
    the King of Hungary's!

SECOND GENTLEMAN Amen.

LUCIO Thou conclud'st like the sanctimonious pirate,
    that went to sea with the Ten Commandments, but
    scraped one out of the table.

10 SECOND GENTLEMAN 'Thou shalt not steal'?

LUCIO Ay, that he razed.

FIRST GENTLEMAN Why, 'twas a commandment to
    command the captain and all the rest from their func-
    tions. They put forth to steal. There's not a soldier of
    us all that, in the thanksgiving before meat, do relish the
    petition well that prays for peace.

SECOND GENTLEMAN I never heard any soldier dislike it.

LUCIO I believe thee, for I think thou never wast where
    grace was said.

20 SECOND GENTLEMAN No? A dozen times at least.

FIRST GENTLEMAN What? In metre?

LUCIO In any proportion, or in any language.

FIRST GENTLEMAN I think, or in any religion.

LUCIO Ay, why not? Grace is grace, despite of all controversy; as, for example, thou thyself art a wicked villain, despite of all grace.

FIRST GENTLEMAN Well, there went but a pair of shears between us.

LUCIO I grant: as there may between the lists and the velvet. Thou art the list.   30

FIRST GENTLEMAN And thou the velvet. Thou art good velvet. Thou'rt a three-piled piece, I warrant thee. I had as lief be a list of an English kersey as be piled, as thou art piled, for a French velvet. Do I speak feelingly now?

LUCIO I think thou dost, and indeed with most painful feeling of thy speech. I will, out of thine own confession, learn to begin thy health, but, whilst I live, forget to drink after thee.

FIRST GENTLEMAN I think I have done myself wrong,   40
have I not?

SECOND GENTLEMAN Yes, that thou hast, whether thou art tainted or free.

Enter Mistress Overdone

LUCIO Behold, behold, where Madam Mitigation comes. I have purchased as many diseases under her roof as come to –

SECOND GENTLEMAN To what, I pray?

LUCIO Judge.

SECOND GENTLEMAN To three thousand dolours a year.

FIRST GENTLEMAN Ay, and more.   50

LUCIO A French crown more.

FIRST GENTLEMAN Thou art always figuring diseases in me, but thou art full of error. I am sound.

LUCIO Nay, not, as one would say, healthy, but so sound
as things that are hollow. Thy bones are hollow.
Impiety has made a feast of thee.

FIRST GENTLEMAN How now, which of your hips has
the most profound sciatica?

MISTRESS OVERDONE Well, well; there's one yonder
60   arrested and carried to prison was worth five thousand
of you all.

SECOND GENTLEMAN Who's that, I pray thee?

MISTRESS OVERDONE Marry, sir, that's Claudio, Signor
Claudio.

FIRST GENTLEMAN Claudio to prison? 'Tis not so.

MISTRESS OVERDONE Nay, but I know 'tis so. I saw him
arrested, saw him carried away, and, which is more,
within these three days his head to be chopped off.

LUCIO But, after all this fooling, I would not have it so.
70   Art thou sure of this?

MISTRESS OVERDONE I am too sure of it; and it is for
getting Madam Julietta with child.

LUCIO Believe me, this may be. He promised to meet me
two hours since, and he was ever precise in promise-
keeping.

SECOND GENTLEMAN Besides, you know, it draws
something near to the speech we had to such a purpose.

FIRST GENTLEMAN But most of all agreeing with the
proclamation.

80   LUCIO Away. Let's go learn the truth of it.

Exeunt Lucio and Gentlemen

MISTRESS OVERDONE Thus, what with the war, what with
the sweat, what with the gallows, and what with
poverty, I am custom-shrunk.

Enter Pompey

How now? What's the news with you?

POMPEY Yonder man is carried to prison.

MISTRESS OVERDONE Well, what has he done?

POMPEY A woman.

MISTRESS OVERDONE But what's his offence?

POMPEY Groping for trouts in a peculiar river.

MISTRESS OVERDONE What? Is there a maid with child   90
by him?

POMPEY No, but there's a woman with maid by him. You
have not heard of the proclamation, have you?

MISTRESS OVERDONE What proclamation, man?

POMPEY All houses in the suburbs of Vienna must be
plucked down.

MISTRESS OVERDONE And what shall become of those
in the city?

POMPEY They shall stand for seed. They had gone down
too, but that a wise burgher put in for them.   100

MISTRESS OVERDONE But shall all our houses of resort
in the suburbs be pulled down?

POMPEY To the ground, mistress.

MISTRESS OVERDONE Why, here's a change indeed in
the commonwealth. What shall become of me?

POMPEY Come, fear not you; good counsellors lack no
clients. Though you change your place, you need not
change your trade. I'll be your tapster still. Courage,
there will be pity taken on you. You that have worn your
eyes almost out in the service, you will be considered.   110

MISTRESS OVERDONE What's to do here, Thomas
Tapster? Let's withdraw.

POMPEY Here comes Signor Claudio, led by the provost
to prison; and there's Madam Juliet.   *Exeunt*
Enter Provost, Claudio, Juliet, Officers, Lucio, and
two Gentlemen

CLAUDIO
Fellow, why dost thou show me thus to th'world?
Bear me to prison, where I am committed.

PROVOST
    I do it not in evil disposition,
    But from Lord Angelo by special charge.

CLAUDIO
    Thus can the demigod Authority
120   Make us pay down for our offence by weight
    The words of heaven. On whom it will, it will;
    On whom it will not, so: yet still 'tis just.

LUCIO
    Why, how now, Claudio? Whence comes this restraint?

CLAUDIO
    From too much liberty, my Lucio, liberty.
    As surfeit is the father of much fast,
    So every scope by the immoderate use
    Turns to restraint. Our natures do pursue,
    Like rats that ravin down their proper bane,
    A thirsty evil, and when we drink we die.

130 LUCIO If I could speak so wisely under an arrest, I would
    send for certain of my creditors. And yet, to say the
    truth, I had as lief have the foppery of freedom as
    the mortality of imprisonment. What's thy offence,
    Claudio?

CLAUDIO What but to speak of would offend again.

LUCIO What, is't murder?

CLAUDIO No.

LUCIO Lechery?

CLAUDIO Call it so.

140 PROVOST Away, sir, you must go.

CLAUDIO One word, good friend. Lucio, a word with you.

LUCIO
    A hundred, if they'll do you any good.
    Is lechery so looked after?

CLAUDIO
    Thus stands it with me: upon a true contract

I got possession of Julietta's bed.
You know the lady. She is fast my wife
Save that we do the denunciation lack
Of outward order. This we came not to,
Only for propagation of a dower
Remaining in the coffer of her friends,   150
From whom we thought it meet to hide our love
Till time had made them for us. But it chances
The stealth of our most mutual entertainment
With character too gross is writ on Juliet.

LUCIO

With child, perhaps?

CLAUDIO   Unhappily, even so.
And the new deputy now for the Duke –
Whether it be the fault and glimpse of newness,
Or whether that the body public be
A horse whereon the governor doth ride,
Who, newly in the seat, that it may know   160
He can command, lets it straight feel the spur;
Whether the tyranny be in his place,
Or in his eminence that fills it up,
I stagger in – but this new governor
Awakes me all the enrollèd penalties
Which have, like unscoured armour, hung by th'wall
So long that nineteen zodiacs have gone round
And none of them been worn, and for a name
Now puts the drowsy and neglected act
Freshly on me. 'Tis surely for a name.   170

LUCIO I warrant it is; and thy head stands so tickle on thy
shoulders that a milkmaid, if she be in love, may sithe it
off. Send after the Duke and appeal to him.

CLAUDIO

I have done so, but he's not to be found.
I prithee, Lucio, do me this kind service:

This day my sister should the cloister enter,
And there receive her approbation.
Acquaint her with the danger of my state,
Implore her, in my voice, that she make friends
180   To the strict deputy, bid herself assay him.
I have great hope in that, for in her youth
There is a prone and speechless dialect,
Such as move men; beside, she hath prosperous art
When she will play with reason and discourse,
And well she can persuade.

LUCIO I pray she may, as well for the encouragement of the
like, which else would stand under grievous imposition,
as for the enjoying of thy life, who I would be sorry
should be thus foolishly lost at a game of tick-tack.
190   I'll to her.

CLAUDIO
I thank you, good friend Lucio.

LUCIO
Within two hours.

CLAUDIO   Come, officer, away.   *Exeunt*

I.3   *Enter Duke and Friar Thomas*

DUKE
No, holy father, throw away that thought;
Believe not that the dribbling dart of love
Can pierce a complete bosom. Why I desire thee
To give me secret harbour hath a purpose
More grave and wrinkled than the aims and ends
Of burning youth.

FRIAR THOMAS   May your grace speak of it?

DUKE
My holy sir, none better knows than you
How I have ever loved the life removed

And held in idle price to haunt assemblies
Where youth and cost a witless bravery keeps.   10
I have delivered to Lord Angelo,
A man of stricture and firm abstinence,
My absolute power and place here in Vienna,
And he supposes me travelled to Poland,
For so I have strewed it in the common ear,
And so it is received. Now, pious sir,
You will demand of me why I do this.

FRIAR THOMAS
Gladly, my lord.

DUKE
We have strict statutes and most biting laws,
The needful bits and curbs to headstrong weeds,   20
Which for this fourteen years we have let slip;
Even like an o'ergrown lion in a cave,
That goes not out to prey. Now, as fond fathers,
Having bound up the threatening twigs of birch,
Only to stick it in their children's sight
For terror, not to use, in time the rod
Becomes more mocked than feared, so our decrees,
Dead to infliction, to themselves are dead,
And liberty plucks justice by the nose;
The baby beats the nurse, and quite athwart   30
Goes all decorum.

FRIAR THOMAS   It rested in your grace
To unloose this tied-up justice when you pleased,
And it in you more dreadful would have seemed
Than in Lord Angelo.

DUKE   I do fear, too dreadful.
Sith 'twas my fault to give the people scope,
'Twould be my tyranny to strike and gall them
For what I bid them do: for we bid this be done
When evil deeds have their permissive pass

And not the punishment. Therefore, indeed, my father,
40   I have on Angelo imposed the office,
Who may, in th'ambush of my name, strike home,
And yet my nature never in the fight
To do it slander. And to behold his sway
I will, as 'twere a brother of your order,
Visit both prince and people. Therefore, I prithee,
Supply me with the habit, and instruct me
How I may formally in person bear
Like a true friar. More reasons for this action
At our more leisure shall I render you;
50   Only this one – Lord Angelo is precise,
Stands at a guard with envy, scarce confesses
That his blood flows, or that his appetite
Is more to bread than stone. Hence shall we see,
If power change purpose, what our seemers be. *Exeunt*

I.4   *Enter Isabella and Francisca, a nun*

ISABELLA
And have you nuns no farther privileges?

FRANCISCA
Are not these large enough?

ISABELLA
Yes, truly. I speak not as desiring more,
But rather wishing a more strict restraint
Upon the sisterhood, the votarists of Saint Clare.
    Lucio within

LUCIO
Ho! Peace be in this place.

ISABELLA   Who's that which calls?

FRANCISCA
It is a man's voice. Gentle Isabella,
Turn you the key, and know his business of him.

You may, I may not; you are yet unsworn.
When you have vowed, you must not speak with men   10
But in the presence of the prioress;
Then, if you speak, you must not show your face,
Or, if you show your face, you must not speak.
He calls again. I pray you, answer him.   *Exit*

ISABELLA

Peace and prosperity! Who is't that calls?
    Enter Lucio

LUCIO

Hail, virgin, if you be, as those cheek-roses
Proclaim you are no less. Can you so stead me
As bring me to the sight of Isabella,
A novice of this place, and the fair sister
To her unhappy brother, Claudio?   20

ISABELLA

Why 'her unhappy brother'? Let me ask,
The rather for I now must make you know
I am that Isabella, and his sister.

LUCIO

Gentle and fair, your brother kindly greets you.
Not to be weary with you, he's in prison.

ISABELLA

Woe me, for what?

LUCIO

For that which, if myself might be his judge,
He should receive his punishment in thanks.
He hath got his friend with child.

ISABELLA

Sir, make me not your story.

LUCIO   'Tis true.   30
I would not, though 'tis my familiar sin
With maids to seem the lapwing and to jest,
Tongue far from heart, play with all virgins so.

I hold you as a thing enskied and sainted,
By your renouncement an immortal spirit
And to be talked with in sincerity,
As with a saint.

ISABELLA

You do blaspheme the good in mocking me.

LUCIO

Do not believe it. Fewness and truth, 'tis thus:
40   Your brother and his lover have embraced.
As those that feed grow full, as blossoming time
That from the seedness the bare fallow brings
To teeming foison, even so her plenteous womb
Expresseth his full tilth and husbandry.

ISABELLA

Someone with child by him? My cousin Juliet?

LUCIO

Is she your cousin?

ISABELLA

Adoptedly, as school-maids change their names
By vain though apt affection.

LUCIO   She it is.

ISABELLA O, let him marry her.

LUCIO   This the point.
50   The Duke is very strangely gone from hence,
Bore many gentlemen, myself being one,
In hand and hope of action; but we do learn
By those that know the very nerves of state,
His giving-out were of an infinite distance
From his true-meant design. Upon his place,
And with full line of his authority,
Governs Lord Angelo, a man whose blood
Is very snow-broth, one who never feels
The wanton stings and motions of the sense,
60   But doth rebate and blunt his natural edge

With profits of the mind, study, and fast.
He, to give fear to use and liberty,
Which have for long run by the hideous law,
As mice by lions, hath picked out an act,
Under whose heavy sense your brother's life
Falls into forfeit; he arrests him on it,
And follows close the rigour of the statute
To make him an example. All hope is gone,
Unless you have the grace by your fair prayer
To soften Angelo. And that's my pith of business   70
'Twixt you and your poor brother.

ISABELLA
Doth he so seek his life?

LUCIO   Has censured him
Already and, as I hear, the provost hath
A warrant for's execution.

ISABELLA
Alas, what poor ability's in me
To do him good.

LUCIO   Assay the power you have.

ISABELLA
My power? Alas, I doubt.

LUCIO   Our doubts are traitors
And makes us lose the good we oft might win,
By fearing to attempt. Go to Lord Angelo,
And let him learn to know, when maidens sue,   80
Men give like gods; but when they weep and kneel,
All their petitions are as freely theirs
As they themselves would owe them.

ISABELLA
I'll see what I can do.

LUCIO   But speedily.

ISABELLA
I will about it straight,

No longer staying but to give the Mother
Notice of my affair. I humbly thank you.
Commend me to my brother. Soon at night
I'll send him certain word of my success.

LUCIO

90   I take my leave of you.

ISABELLA   Good sir, adieu.   *Exeunt*

*

II.I   *Enter Angelo, Escalus, and Servants, Justice*

ANGELO
We must not make a scarecrow of the law,
Setting it up to fear the birds of prey,
And let it keep one shape, till custom make it
Their perch and not their terror.

ESCALUS   Ay, but yet
Let us be keen and rather cut a little
Than fall, and bruise to death. Alas, this gentleman,
Whom I would save, had a most noble father.
Let but your honour know,
Whom I believe to be most strait in virtue,
10   That, in the working of your own affections,
Had time cohered with place or place with wishing,
Or that the resolute acting of your blood
Could have attained th'effect of your own purpose,
Whether you had not sometime in your life
Erred in this point which now you censure him,
And pulled the law upon you.

ANGELO
'Tis one thing to be tempted, Escalus,
Another thing to fall. I not deny,
The jury passing on the prisoner's life,

May in the sworn twelve have a thief or two   20
Guiltier than him they try; what's open made to justice,
That justice seizes; what knows the laws
That thieves do pass on thieves? 'Tis very pregnant,
The jewel that we find, we stoop and take't
Because we see it; but what we do not see
We tread upon, and never think of it.
You may not so extenuate his offence
For I have had such faults; but rather tell me,
When I, that censure him, do so offend,
Let mine own judgement pattern out my death   30
And nothing come in partial. Sir, he must die.

    Enter Provost

ESCALUS

Be it as your wisdom will.

ANGELO   Where is the provost?

PROVOST

Here, if it like your honour.

ANGELO   See that Claudio
Be execute by nine tomorrow morning:
Bring him his confessor, let him be prepared;
For that's the utmost of his pilgrimage.   *Exit Provost*

ESCALUS

Well, heaven forgive him, and forgive us all.
Some rise by sin, and some by virtue fall:
Some run from brakes of vice, and answer none,
And some condemnèd for a fault alone.   40

    Enter Elbow, Froth, Pompey, Officers

ELBOW Come, bring them away. If these be good people
in a commonweal that do nothing but use their abuses
in common houses, I know no law. Bring them away.

ANGELO How now, sir, what's your name? And what's
the matter?

ELBOW If it please your honour, I am the poor Duke's

constable, and my name is Elbow. I do lean upon
justice, sir, and do bring in here before your good
honour two notorious benefactors.

50 ANGELO Benefactors? Well, what benefactors are they?
Are they not malefactors?

ELBOW If it please your honour, I know not well what they
are; but precise villains they are, that I am sure of, and
void of all profanation in the world that good Christians
ought to have.

ESCALUS This comes off well. Here's a wise officer.

ANGELO Go to. What quality are they of? Elbow is your
name? Why dost thou not speak, Elbow?

POMPEY He cannot, sir. He's out at elbow.

60 ANGELO What are you, sir?

ELBOW He, sir? A tapster, sir, parcel-bawd; one that
serves a bad woman, whose house, sir, was, as they say,
plucked down in the suburbs, and now she professes a
hot-house, which I think is a very ill house too.

ESCALUS How know you that?

ELBOW My wife, sir, whom I detest before heaven and
your honour –

ESCALUS How? Thy wife?

ELBOW Ay, sir, whom I thank heaven is an honest
70 woman –

ESCALUS Dost thou detest her therefore?

ELBOW I say, sir, I will detest myself also, as well as she,
that this house, if it be not a bawd's house, it is pity
of her life, for it is a naughty house.

ESCALUS How dost thou know that, constable?

ELBOW Marry, sir, by my wife, who, if she had been a
woman cardinally given, might have been accused in
fornication, adultery, and all uncleanliness there.

ESCALUS By the woman's means?

80 ELBOW Ay, sir, by Mistress Overdone's means; but as

she spit in his face, so she defied him.

POMPEY Sir, if it please your honour, this is not so.

ELBOW Prove it before these varlets here, thou honourable man, prove it.

ESCALUS Do you hear how he misplaces?

POMPEY Sir, she came in great with child, and longing –
saving your honour's reverence – for stewed prunes.
Sir, we had but two in the house, which at that very
distant time stood, as it were, in a fruit dish, a dish of
some threepence; your honours have seen such dishes;   90
they are not china dishes, but very good dishes.

ESCALUS Go to, go to; no matter for the dish, sir.

POMPEY No, indeed, sir, not of a pin; you are therein in
the right: but to the point. As I say, this Mistress
Elbow, being, as I say, with child, and being great-
bellied, and longing, as I said, for prunes, and having
but two in the dish, as I said, Master Froth here, this
very man, having eaten the rest, as I said, and, as I
say, paying for them very honestly, for, as you know,
Master Froth, I could not give you threepence again.   100

FROTH No, indeed.

POMPEY Very well: you being then, if you be remembered, cracking the stones of the foresaid prunes –

FROTH Ay, so I did, indeed.

POMPEY Why, very well: I telling you then, if you be remembered, that such a one and such a one were past
cure of the thing you wot of, unless they kept very good
diet, as I told you –

FROTH All this is true.

POMPEY Why, very well then –   110

ESCALUS Come, you are a tedious fool. To the purpose.
What was done to Elbow's wife, that he hath cause to
complain of? Come me to what was done to her.

POMPEY Sir, your honour cannot come to that yet.

ESCALUS No, sir, nor I mean it not.

POMPEY Sir, but you shall come to it, by your honour's
leave. And I beseech you look into Master Froth here,
sir; a man of fourscore pound a year, whose father died
at Hallowmas. Was't not at Hallowmas, Master Froth?

120 FROTH Allhallond Eve.

POMPEY Why, very well. I hope here be truths. He, sir,
sitting, as I say, in a lower chair, sir — 'twas in the
Bunch of Grapes, where indeed you have a delight to sit,
have you not?

FROTH I have so, because it is an open room and good for
winter.

POMPEY Why, very well then. I hope here be truths.

ANGELO
This will last out a night in Russia
When nights are longest there. I'll take my leave,
130 And leave you to the hearing of the cause,
Hoping you'll find good cause to whip them all.

ESCALUS I think no less. Good morrow to your lordship.

                      Exit Angelo

Now, sir, come on. What was done to Elbow's wife,
once more?

POMPEY Once, sir? There was nothing done to her once.

ELBOW I beseech you, sir, ask him what this man did to
my wife.

POMPEY I beseech your honour, ask me.

ESCALUS Well, sir, what did this gentleman to her?

140 POMPEY I beseech you, sir, look in this gentleman's face.
Good Master Froth, look upon his honour; 'tis for a
good purpose. Doth your honour mark his face?

ESCALUS Ay, sir, very well.

POMPEY Nay, I beseech you, mark it well.

ESCALUS Well, I do so.

POMPEY Doth your honour see any harm in his face?

ESCALUS Why, no.

POMPEY I'll be supposed upon a book, his face is the
worst thing about him. Good then; if his face be the
worst thing about him, how could Master Froth do the   150
constable's wife any harm? I would know that of your
honour.

ESCALUS He's in the right. Constable, what say you to it?

ELBOW First, an it like you, the house is a respected
house; next, this is a respected fellow, and his mistress
is a respected woman.

POMPEY By this hand, sir, his wife is a more respected
person than any of us all.

ELBOW Varlet, thou liest; thou liest, wicked varlet. The
time is yet to come that she was ever respected with man,   160
woman, or child.

POMPEY Sir, she was respected with him before he
married with her.

ESCALUS Which is the wiser here, Justice or Iniquity? Is
this true?

ELBOW O thou caitiff, O thou varlet, O thou wicked
Hannibal! I respected with her before I was married
to her? If ever I was respected with her, or she with
me, let not your worship think me the poor Duke's
officer. Prove this, thou wicked Hannibal, or I'll have   170
mine action of battery on thee.

ESCALUS If he took you a box o'th'ear, you might have
your action of slander, too.

ELBOW Marry, I thank your good worship for it. What
is't your worship's pleasure I shall do with this wicked
caitiff?

ESCALUS Truly, officer, because he hath some offences in
him that thou wouldst discover, if thou couldst, let him
continue in his courses till thou know'st what they are.

ELBOW Marry, I thank your worship for it. Thou seest,   180

thou wicked varlet, now, what's come upon thee. Thou
art to continue now, thou varlet, thou art to continue.

ESCALUS Where were you born, friend?

FROTH Here in Vienna, sir.

ESCALUS Are you of fourscore pounds a year?

FROTH Yes, an't please you, sir.

ESCALUS So. What trade are you of, sir?

POMPEY A tapster, a poor widow's tapster.

ESCALUS Your mistress' name?

190 POMPEY Mistress Overdone.

ESCALUS Hath she had any more than one husband?

POMPEY Nine, sir. Overdone by the last.

ESCALUS Nine? Come hither to me, Master Froth.
Master Froth, I would not have you acquainted with
tapsters; they will draw you, Master Froth, and you will
hang them. Get you gone, and let me hear no more of
you.

FROTH I thank your worship. For mine own part, I
never come into any room in a taphouse but I am drawn
200 in.

ESCALUS Well, no more of it, Master Froth. Farewell.

Exit Froth

Come you hither to me, Master Tapster. What's your
name, Master Tapster?

POMPEY Pompey.

ESCALUS What else?

POMPEY Bum, sir.

ESCALUS Troth, and your bum is the greatest thing about
you, so that, in the beastliest sense, you are Pompey the
Great. Pompey, you are partly a bawd, Pompey, how-
210 soever you colour it in being a tapster, are you not?
Come, tell me true. It shall be the better for you.

POMPEY Truly, sir, I am a poor fellow that would live.

ESCALUS How would you live, Pompey? By being a

bawd? What do you think of the trade, Pompey? Is it a
lawful trade?

POMPEY If the law would allow it, sir.

ESCALUS But the law will not allow it, Pompey; nor it
shall not be allowed in Vienna.

POMPEY Does your worship mean to geld and splay all
the youth of the city?   220

ESCALUS No, Pompey.

POMPEY Truly, sir, in my poor opinion, they will to't
then. If your worship will take order for the drabs and
the knaves, you need not to fear the bawds.

ESCALUS There is pretty orders beginning, I can tell you.
It is but heading and hanging.

POMPEY If you head and hang all that offend that way
but for ten year together, you'll be glad to give out a
commission for more heads. If this law hold in Vienna
ten year, I'll rent the fairest house in it after threepence   230
a bay. If you live to see this come to pass, say Pompey
told you so.

ESCALUS Thank you, good Pompey, and, in requital of
your prophecy, hark you: I advise you, let me not find
you before me again upon any complaint whatsoever;
no, not for dwelling where you do. If I do, Pompey, I
shall beat you to your tent, and prove a shrewd Caesar
to you. In plain dealing, Pompey, I shall have you
whipped. So, for this time, Pompey, fare you well.

POMPEY I thank your worship for your good counsel;   240
but I shall follow it as the flesh and fortune shall better
determine.

Whip me? No, no, let carman whip his jade.

The valiant heart's not whipped out of his trade. *Exit*

ESCALUS Come hither to me, Master Elbow. Come
hither, master constable. How long have you been in
this place of constable?

ELBOW Seven year and a half, sir.

ESCALUS I thought, by the readiness in the office, you had
continued in it some time. You say, seven years together?

ELBOW And a half, sir.

ESCALUS Alas, it hath been great pains to you; they do
you wrong to put you so oft upon't. Are there not men in
your ward sufficient to serve it?

ELBOW Faith, sir, few of any wit in such matters. As they
are chosen, they are glad to choose me for them. I do it
for some piece of money, and go through with all.

ESCALUS Look you bring me in the names of some six or
seven, the most sufficient of your parish.

ELBOW To your worship's house, sir?

ESCALUS To my house. Fare you well.   *Exit Elbow*
What's o'clock, think you?

JUSTICE Eleven, sir.

ESCALUS I pray you home to dinner with me.

JUSTICE I humbly thank you.

ESCALUS
It grieves me for the death of Claudio,
But there's no remedy.

JUSTICE
Lord Angelo is severe.

ESCALUS   It is but needful.
Mercy is not itself, that oft looks so;
Pardon is still the nurse of second woe.
But yet poor Claudio; there is no remedy.
Come, sir.   *Exeunt*

Enter Provost, and a Servant

SERVANT
He's hearing of a cause; he will come straight;
I'll tell him of you.

PROVOST   Pray you, do.   *Exit Servant*
                         I'll know
His pleasure; maybe he will relent. Alas,
He hath but as offended in a dream.
All sects, all ages smack of this vice, and he
To die for't!
     Enter Angelo

ANGELO   Now, what's the matter, provost?

PROVOST
Is it your will Claudio shall die tomorrow?

ANGELO
Did not I tell thee, yea? Hadst thou not order?
Why dost thou ask again?

PROVOST   Lest I might be too rash.
Under your good correction, I have seen   10
When, after execution, judgement hath
Repented o'er his doom.

ANGELO   Go to; let that be mine.
Do you your office, or give up your place,
And you shall well be spared.

PROVOST   I crave your honour's pardon.
What shall be done, sir, with the groaning Juliet?
She's very near her hour.

ANGELO   Dispose of her
To some more fitter place, and that with speed.
     Enter Servant

SERVANT
Here is the sister of the man condemned
Desires access to you.

ANGELO   Hath he a sister?

PROVOST

20   Ay, my good lord, a very virtuous maid,
And to be shortly of a sisterhood,
If not already.

ANGELO   Well, let her be admitted.   *Exit Servant*
See you the fornicatress be removed;
Let her have needful, but not lavish, means.
There shall be order for't.

     Enter Lucio and Isabella

PROVOST   God save your honour.

ANGELO

Stay a little while. (*To Isabella*) Y'are welcome. What's
your will?

ISABELLA

I am a woeful suitor to your honour,
Please but your honour hear me.

ANGELO   Well, what's your suit?

ISABELLA

There is a vice that most I do abhor,
30   And most desire should meet the blow of justice,
For which I would not plead, but that I must,
For which I must not plead, but that I am
At war 'twixt will and will not.

ANGELO   Well: the matter?

ISABELLA

I have a brother is condemned to die.
I do beseech you, let it be his fault,
And not my brother.

PROVOST (*aside*)   Heaven give thee moving graces.

ANGELO

Condemn the fault, and not the actor of it?
Why, every fault's condemned ere it be done.
Mine were the very cipher of a function,

To fine the faults whose fine stands in record,   40
And let go by the actor.
ISABELLA   O just, but severe law!
  I had a brother then; heaven keep your honour.
LUCIO (*aside to Isabella*)
  Give't not o'er so. To him again, entreat him,
  Kneel down before him, hang upon his gown;
  You are too cold. If you should need a pin,
  You could not with more tame a tongue desire it.
  To him, I say.
ISABELLA
  Must he needs die?
ANGELO   Maiden, no remedy.
ISABELLA
  Yes, I do think that you might pardon him,
  And neither heaven nor man grieve at the mercy.   50
ANGELO
  I will not do't.
ISABELLA   But can you if you would?
ANGELO
  Look what I will not, that I cannot do.
ISABELLA
  But might you do't, and do the world no wrong,
  If so your heart were touched with that remorse
  As mine is to him?
ANGELO
  He's sentenced; 'tis too late.
LUCIO (*aside to Isabella*)   You are too cold.
ISABELLA
  Too late? Why, no. I that do speak a word
  May call it again. Well, believe this,
  No ceremony that to great ones longs,
  Not the king's crown, nor the deputed sword,   60

The marshal's truncheon, nor the judge's robe,
Become them with one half so good a grace
As mercy does.
If he had been as you, and you as he,
You would have slipped like him; but he, like you,
Would not have been so stern.

ANGELO   Pray you, be gone.

ISABELLA

I would to heaven I had your potency,
And you were Isabel; should it then be thus?
No, I would tell what 'twere to be a judge,
70   And what a prisoner.

LUCIO (*aside to Isabella*)

                          Ay, touch him; there's the vein.

ANGELO

Your brother is a forfeit of the law,
And you but waste your words.

ISABELLA   Alas, alas;

Why, all the souls that were were forfeit once,
And He that might the vantage best have took
Found out the remedy. How would you be,
If He, which is the top of judgement, should
But judge you as you are? O think on that,
And mercy then will breathe within your lips,
Like man new made.

ANGELO   Be you content, fair maid,
80   It is the law, not I, condemn your brother;
Were he my kinsman, brother, or my son,
It should be thus with him. He must die tomorrow.

ISABELLA

Tomorrow? O, that's sudden; spare him, spare him.
He's not prepared for death. Even for our kitchens
We kill the fowl of season. Shall we serve heaven
With less respect than we do minister

To our gross selves? Good, good my lord, bethink you:
Who is it that hath died for this offence?
There's many have committed it.

LUCIO (*aside to Isabella*)   Ay, well said.

ANGELO

The law hath not been dead, though it hath slept.   90
Those many had not dared to do that evil
If the first that did th'edict infringe
Had answered for his deed. Now 'tis awake,
Takes note of what is done, and like a prophet
Looks in a glass that shows what future evils,
Either now, or by remissness, new-conceived,
And so in progress to be hatched and born,
Are now to have no successive degrees,
But where they live, to end.

ISABELLA   Yet show some pity.

ANGELO

I show it most of all when I show justice,   100
For then I pity those I do not know,
Which a dismissed offence would after gall,
And do him right that, answering one foul wrong,
Lives not to act another. Be satisfied
Your brother dies tomorrow. Be content.

ISABELLA

So you must be the first that gives this sentence,
And he, that suffers. O, it is excellent
To have a giant's strength, but it is tyrannous
To use it like a giant.

LUCIO (*aside to Isabella*) That's well said.

ISABELLA

Could great men thunder   110
As Jove himself does, Jove would never be quiet,
For every pelting, petty officer
Would use his heaven for thunder,

Nothing but thunder. Merciful heaven,
Thou rather with thy sharp and sulphurous bolt
Splits the unwedgeable and gnarlèd oak
Than the soft myrtle; but man, proud man,
Dressed in a little brief authority,
Most ignorant of what he's most assured,
His glassy essence, like an angry ape
Plays such fantastic tricks before high heaven
As makes the angels weep; who, with our spleens,
Would all themselves laugh mortal.

LUCIO (*aside to Isabella*)

O, to him, to him, wench; he will relent.
He's coming, I perceive't.

PROVOST (*aside*)   Pray heaven she win him.

ISABELLA

We cannot weigh our brother with ourself.
Great men may jest with saints: 'tis wit in them,
But in the less, foul profanation.

LUCIO (*aside to Isabella*)

Thou'rt i'th'right, girl, more o'that.

ISABELLA

That in the captain's but a choleric word
Which in the soldier is flat blasphemy.

LUCIO (*aside to Isabella*)

Art avised o'that? More on't.

ANGELO

Why do you put these sayings upon me?

ISABELLA

Because authority, though it err like others,
Hath yet a kind of medicine in itself
That skins the vice o'th'top. Go to your bosom,
Knock there, and ask your heart what it doth know
That's like my brother's fault; if it confess
A natural guiltiness such as is his,

Let it not sound a thought upon your tongue   140
Against my brother's life.

ANGELO (*aside*)   She speaks, and 'tis
Such sense that my sense breeds with it. Fare you well.

ISABELLA
Gentle my lord, turn back.

ANGELO
I will bethink me. Come again tomorrow.

ISABELLA
Hark how I'll bribe you. Good my lord, turn back.

ANGELO
How? Bribe me?

ISABELLA
Ay, with such gifts that heaven shall share with you.

LUCIO (*aside to Isabella*)
You had marred all else.

ISABELLA
Not with fond sicles of the tested gold,
Or stones whose rate are either rich or poor   150
As fancy values them; but with true prayers
That shall be up at heaven and enter there
Ere sunrise: prayers from preservèd souls,
From fasting maids whose minds are dedicate
To nothing temporal.

ANGELO   Well, come to me tomorrow.

LUCIO (*aside to Isabella*)
Go to, 'tis well; away.

ISABELLA
Heaven keep your honour safe.

ANGELO (*aside*)   Amen.
For I am that way going to temptation,
Where prayers cross.

ISABELLA   At what hour tomorrow
Shall I attend your lordship?   160

ANGELO   At any time 'forenoon.

ISABELLA

God save your honour.

           Exeunt Isabella, Lucio, and Provost

ANGELO   From thee: even from thy virtue.
What's this? What's this? Is this her fault or mine?
The tempter, or the tempted, who sins most?
Ha?
Not she, nor doth she tempt; but it is I
That, lying by the violet in the sun,
Do as the carrion does, not as the flower,
Corrupt with virtuous season. Can it be
That modesty may more betray our sense
170 Than woman's lightness? Having waste ground enough,
Shall we desire to raze the sanctuary
And pitch our evils there? O fie, fie, fie!
What dost thou? Or what art thou, Angelo?
Dost thou desire her foully for those things
That make her good? O, let her brother live:
Thieves for their robbery have authority
When judges steal themselves. What, do I love her,
That I desire to hear her speak again,
And feast upon her eyes? What is't I dream on?
180 O cunning enemy that, to catch a saint,
With saints dost bait thy hook. Most dangerous
Is that temptation that doth goad us on
To sin in loving virtue. Never could the strumpet
With all her double vigour, art and nature,
Once stir my temper; but this virtuous maid
Subdues me quite. Ever till now,
When men were fond, I smiled and wondered how.

                    Exit

Enter Duke, disguised as a friar, and Provost   II.3

DUKE

Hail to you, provost – so I think you are.

PROVOST

I am the provost. What's your will, good friar?

DUKE

Bound by my charity and my blessed order,
I come to visit the afflicted spirits
Here in the prison. Do me the common right
To let me see them and to make me know
The nature of their crimes, that I may minister
To them accordingly.

PROVOST

I would do more than that, if more were needful.
   Enter Juliet
Look, here comes one: a gentlewoman of mine,   10
Who, falling in the flaws of her own youth,
Hath blistered her report. She is with child,
And he that got it, sentenced: a young man
More fit to do another such offence
Than die for this.

DUKE

When must he die?

PROVOST   As I do think, tomorrow.
   (*To Juliet*) I have provided for you; stay a while
And you shall be conducted.

DUKE

Repent you, fair one, of the sin you carry?

JULIET

I do, and bear the shame most patiently.   20

DUKE

I'll teach you how you shall arraign your conscience
And try your penitence, if it be sound,
Or hollowly put on.

JULIET   I'll gladly learn.

DUKE

Love you the man that wronged you?

JULIET

Yes, as I love the woman that wronged him.

DUKE

So then it seems your most offenceful act
Was mutually committed?

JULIET   Mutually.

DUKE

Then was your sin of heavier kind than his.

JULIET

I do confess it, and repent it, father.

DUKE

30   'Tis meet so, daughter, but least you do repent
As that the sin hath brought you to this shame,
Which sorrow is always toward ourselves, not heaven,
Showing we would not spare heaven as we love it,
But as we stand in fear.

JULIET

I do repent me as it is an evil,
And take the shame with joy.

DUKE   There rest.
Your partner, as I hear, must die tomorrow,
And I am going with instruction to him.
Grace go with you. *Benedicite*.   *Exit*

JULIET

40   Must die tomorrow? O injurious love,
That respites me a life whose very comfort
Is still a dying horror.

PROVOST   'Tis pity of him.   *Exeunt*

Enter Angelo   II.4

ANGELO

    When I would pray and think, I think and pray
    To several subjects: heaven hath my empty words,
    Whilst my invention, hearing not my tongue,
    Anchors on Isabel: God in my mouth,
    As if I did but only chew His name,
    And in my heart the strong and swelling evil
    Of my conception. The state, whereon I studied,
    Is like a good thing, being often read,
    Grown seared and tedious; yea, my gravity,
    Wherein, let no man hear me, I take pride,   10
    Could I, with boot, change for an idle plume
    Which the air beats for vain. O place, O form,
    How often dost thou with thy case, thy habit,
    Wrench awe from fools, and tie the wiser souls
    To thy false seeming! Blood, thou art blood;
    Let's write 'good Angel' on the devil's horn,
    'Tis not the devil's crest. How now? Who's there?

    Enter Servant

SERVANT

    One Isabel, a sister, desires access to you.

ANGELO

    Teach her the way.   *Exit Servant*
                O heavens,
    Why does my blood thus muster to my heart,   20
    Making both it unable for itself,
    And dispossessing all my other parts
    Of necessary fitness?
    So play the foolish throngs with one that swoons,
    Come all to help him, and so stop the air
    By which he should revive; and even so
    The general, subject to a well-wished king,
    Quit their own part, and in obsequious fondness

Crowd to his presence, where their untaught love
30   Must needs appear offence.

Enter Isabella

                                  How now, fair maid!

ISABELLA
I am come to know your pleasure.

ANGELO
That you might know it, would much better please me
Than to demand what 'tis. Your brother cannot live.

ISABELLA
Even so. Heaven keep your honour.

ANGELO
Yet may he live a while; and it may be
As long as you or I, yet he must die.

ISABELLA
Under your sentence?

ANGELO
Yea.

ISABELLA
When, I beseech you? That in his reprieve,
40   Longer or shorter, he may be so fitted
That his soul sicken not.

ANGELO
Ha! fie, these filthy vices! It were as good
To pardon him that hath from nature stol'n
A man already made as to remit
Their saucy sweetness that do coin God's image
In stamps that are forbid: 'tis all as easy
Falsely to take away a life true made
As to put metal in restrainèd means
To make a false one.

ISABELLA
50   'Tis set down so in heaven, but not in earth.

ANGELO

    Say you so? Then I shall pose you quickly.
    Which had you rather, that the most just law
    Now took your brother's life, or to redeem him
    Give up your body to such sweet uncleanness
    As she that he hath stained?

ISABELLA   Sir, believe this,

    I had rather give my body than my soul.

ANGELO

    I talk not of your soul. Our compelled sins
    Stand more for number than for accompt.

ISABELLA   How say you?

ANGELO

    Nay, I'll not warrant that, for I can speak
    Against the thing I say. Answer to this: 60
    I, now the voice of the recorded law,
    Pronounce a sentence on your brother's life;
    Might there not be a charity in sin
    To save this brother's life?

ISABELLA   Please you to do't,

    I'll take it as a peril to my soul;
    It is no sin at all, but charity.

ANGELO

    Pleased you to do't, at peril of your soul,
    Were equal poise of sin and charity.

ISABELLA

    That I do beg his life, if it be sin,
    Heaven let me bear it: you granting of my suit,   70
    If that be sin, I'll make it my morn prayer
    To have it added to the faults of mine
    And nothing of your answer.

ANGELO   Nay, but hear me;

    Your sense pursues not mine. Either you are ignorant,
    Or seem so crafty; and that's not good.

ISABELLA

    Let be ignorant, and in nothing good

    But graciously to know I am no better.

ANGELO

    Thus wisdom wishes to appear most bright

    When it doth tax itself, as these black masks

80   Proclaim an enshield beauty ten times louder

    Than beauty could, displayed. But mark me;

    To be receivèd plain, I'll speak more gross:

    Your brother is to die.

ISABELLA

    So.

ANGELO

    And his offence is so, as it appears,

    Accountant to the law upon that pain.

ISABELLA

    True.

ANGELO

    Admit no other way to save his life –

    As I subscribe not that, nor any other,

90   But in the loss of question – that you, his sister,

    Finding yourself desired of such a person

    Whose credit with the judge, or own great place,

    Could fetch your brother from the manacles

    Of the all-binding law; and that there were

    No earthly mean to save him, but that either

    You must lay down the treasures of your body

    To this supposed, or else to let him suffer,

    What would you do?

ISABELLA

    As much for my poor brother as myself:

100   That is, were I under the terms of death,

    Th'impression of keen whips I'd wear as rubies,

    And strip myself to death as to a bed

That longing have been sick for, ere I'd yield
My body up to shame.

ANGELO   Then must your brother die.

ISABELLA

And 'twere the cheaper way.
Better it were a brother died at once
Than that a sister, by redeeming him,
Should die for ever.

ANGELO

Were not you then as cruel as the sentence
That you have slandered so?   110

ISABELLA

Ignomy in ransom and free pardon
Are of two houses: lawful mercy
Is nothing kin to foul redemption.

ANGELO

You seemed of late to make the law a tyrant,
And rather proved the sliding of your brother
A merriment than a vice.

ISABELLA

O pardon me, my lord; it oft falls out
To have what we would have, we speak not what we
     mean.
I something do excuse the thing I hate
For his advantage that I dearly love.   120

ANGELO

We are all frail.

ISABELLA   Else let my brother die,
If not a fedary, but only he
Owe and succeed thy weakness.

ANGELO

Nay, women are frail too.

ISABELLA

Ay, as the glasses where they view themselves,

Which are as easy broke as they make forms.
Women, help heaven! Men their creation mar
In profiting by them. Nay, call us ten times frail,
For we are soft as our complexions are,
And credulous to false prints.

ANGELO   I think it well,
And from this testimony of your own sex –
Since I suppose we are made to be no stronger
Than faults may shake our frames – let me be bold.
I do arrest your words. Be that you are,
That is, a woman; if you be more, you're none.
If you be one, as you are well expressed
By all external warrants, show it now,
By putting on the destined livery.

ISABELLA
I have no tongue but one. Gentle my lord,
Let me entreat you speak the former language.

ANGELO
Plainly conceive, I love you.

ISABELLA
My brother did love Juliet,
And you tell me that he shall die for't.

ANGELO
He shall not, Isabel, if you give me love.

ISABELLA
I know your virtue hath a licence in't,
Which seems a little fouler than it is,
To pluck on others.

ANGELO   Believe me, on mine honour,
My words express my purpose.

ISABELLA
Ha! Little honour to be much believed,
And most pernicious purpose. Seeming, seeming!
I will proclaim thee, Angelo, look for't!

Sign me a present pardon for my brother,
Or with an outstretched throat I'll tell the world
Aloud what man thou art.

ANGELO   Who will believe thee, Isabel?
My unsoiled name, th'austereness of my life,
My vouch against you, and my place i'th'state,
Will so your accusation overweigh
That you shall stifle in your own report
And smell of calumny. I have begun,
And now I give my sensual race the rein.   160
Fit thy consent to my sharp appetite,
Lay by all nicety and prolixious blushes,
That banish what they sue for. Redeem thy brother
By yielding up thy body to my will,
Or else he must not only die the death,
But thy unkindness shall his death draw out
To lingering sufferance. Answer me tomorrow,
Or, by the affection that now guides me most,
I'll prove a tyrant to him. As for you,
Say what you can, my false o'erweighs your true. *Exit*   170

ISABELLA
To whom should I complain? Did I tell this,
Who would believe me? O perilous mouths,
That bear in them one and the selfsame tongue,
Either of condemnation or approof,
Bidding the law make curtsy to their will,
Hooking both right and wrong to th'appetite,
To follow as it draws. I'll to my brother.
Though he hath fall'n by prompture of the blood,
Yet hath he in him such a mind of honour
That, had he twenty heads to tender down   180
On twenty bloody blocks, he'd yield them up,
Before his sister should her body stoop
To such abhorred pollution.

Then, Isabel, live chaste, and, brother, die.
More than our brother is our chastity.
I'll tell him yet of Angelo's request,
And fit his mind to death, for his soul's rest.   *Exit*

*

III.I   *Enter Duke, as a friar, Claudio, and Provost*

DUKE
So then you hope of pardon from Lord Angelo?

CLAUDIO
The miserable have no other medicine
But only hope:
I've hope to live, and am prepared to die.

DUKE
Be absolute for death: either death or life
Shall thereby be the sweeter. Reason thus with life:
If I do lose thee, I do lose a thing
That none but fools would keep; a breath thou art,
Servile to all the skyey influences
That dost this habitation where thou keep'st   10
Hourly afflict. Merely, thou art death's fool,
For him thou labour'st by thy flight to shun,
And yet runn'st toward him still. Thou art not noble,
For all th'accommodations that thou bear'st
Are nursed by baseness. Thou'rt by no means valiant,
For thou dost fear the soft and tender fork
Of a poor worm. Thy best of rest is sleep,
And that thou oft provok'st, yet grossly fear'st
Thy death, which is no more. Thou art not thyself,
For thou exists on many a thousand grains   20
That issue out of dust. Happy thou art not,
For what thou hast not, still thou striv'st to get,

And what thou hast, forget'st. Thou art not certain,
For thy complexion shifts to strange effects,
After the moon. If thou art rich, thou'rt poor,
For, like an ass, whose back with ingots bows,
Thou bear'st thy heavy riches but a journey,
And death unloads thee. Friend hast thou none,
For thine own bowels, which do call thee sire,
The mere effusion of thy proper loins,   30
Do curse the gout, serpigo, and the rheum
For ending thee no sooner. Thou hast nor youth nor age,
But as it were an after-dinner's sleep,
Dreaming on both, for all thy blessed youth
Becomes as agèd, and doth beg the alms
Of palsied eld: and when thou art old and rich,
Thou hast neither heat, affection, limb, nor beauty
To make thy riches pleasant. What's yet in this
That bears the name of life? Yet in this life
Lie hid more thousand deaths; yet death we fear,   40
That makes these odds all even.

CLAUDIO   I humbly thank you.
To sue to live, I find I seek to die,
And, seeking death, find life. Let it come on.
    Enter Isabella

ISABELLA What, ho! Peace here, grace and good company.

PROVOST Who's there? Come in. The wish deserves a welcome.

DUKE Dear sir, ere long I'll visit you again.

CLAUDIO Most holy sir, I thank you.

ISABELLA My business is a word or two with Claudio.   50

PROVOST And very welcome. Look, signor, here's your sister.

DUKE Provost, a word with you.

PROVOST As many as you please.

DUKE Bring me to hear them speak, where I may be concealed.

    Duke and Provost retire

CLAUDIO Now, sister, what's the comfort?

ISABELLA

    Why,

    As all comforts are: most good, most good indeed.

60   Lord Angelo, having affairs to heaven,

    Intends you for his swift ambassador,

    Where you shall be an everlasting leiger.

    Therefore your best appointment make with speed;

    Tomorrow you set on.

CLAUDIO   Is there no remedy?

ISABELLA

    None, but such remedy as, to save a head,

    To cleave a heart in twain.

CLAUDIO   But is there any?

ISABELLA

    Yes, brother, you may live;

    There is a devilish mercy in the judge,

    If you'll implore it, that will free your life,

70   But fetter you till death.

CLAUDIO   Perpetual durance?

ISABELLA

    Ay, just. Perpetual durance, a restraint,

    Though all the world's vastidity you had,

    To a determined scope.

CLAUDIO   But in what nature?

ISABELLA

    In such a one as, you consenting to't,

    Would bark your honour from that trunk you bear,

    And leave you naked.

CLAUDIO   Let me know the point.

ISABELLA

O, I do fear thee, Claudio, and I quake
Lest thou a feverous life shouldst entertain,
And six or seven winters more respect
Than a perpetual honour. Dar'st thou die?   80
The sense of death is most in apprehension,
And the poor beetle that we tread upon
In corporal sufferance finds a pang as great
As when a giant dies.

CLAUDIO   Why give you me this shame?

Think you I can a resolution fetch
From flowery tenderness? If I must die,
I will encounter darkness as a bride,
And hug it in mine arms.

ISABELLA

There spake my brother. There my father's grave
Did utter forth a voice. Yes, thou must die.   90
Thou art too noble to conserve a life
In base appliances. This outward-sainted deputy,
Whose settled visage and deliberate word
Nips youth i'th'head, and follies doth enew
As falcon doth the fowl, is yet a devil.
His filth within being cast, he would appear
A pond as deep as hell.

CLAUDIO   The princely Angelo?

ISABELLA

O, 'tis the cunning livery of hell,
The damnèd'st body to invest and cover
In princely guards. Dost thou think, Claudio,   100
If I would yield him my virginity,
Thou might'st be freed?

CLAUDIO   O heavens, it cannot be.

ISABELLA

Yes, he would give't thee, from this rank offence,

So to offend him still. This night's the time
That I should do what I abhor to name,
Or else thou diest tomorrow.

CLAUDIO   Thou shalt not do't.

ISABELLA

O, were it but my life,
I'd throw it down for your deliverance
As frankly as a pin.

CLAUDIO   Thanks, dear Isabel

ISABELLA

110   Be ready, Claudio, for your death tomorrow.

CLAUDIO

Yes. Has he affections in him
That thus can make him bite the law by th'nose,
When he would force it? Sure it is no sin,
Or of the deadly seven it is the least.

ISABELLA

Which is the least?

CLAUDIO

If it were damnable, he being so wise,
Why would he for the momentary trick
Be perdurably fined? O Isabel!

ISABELLA

What says my brother?

CLAUDIO   Death is a fearful thing.

ISABELLA

120   And shamèd life a hateful.

CLAUDIO

Ay, but to die, and go we know not where,
To lie in cold obstruction and to rot;
This sensible warm motion to become
A kneaded cold; and the delighted spirit
To bathe in fiery floods, or to reside
In thrilling region of thick-ribbèd ice,

To be imprisoned in the viewless winds
And blown with restless violence round about
The pendent world; or to be worse than worst
Of those that lawless and incertain thought   130
Imagine howling, 'tis too horrible.
The weariest and most loathèd worldly life
That age, ache, penury, and imprisonment
Can lay on nature is a paradise
To what we fear of death.

ISABELLA
  Alas, alas.

CLAUDIO   Sweet sister, let me live.
  What sin you do to save a brother's life,
  Nature dispenses with the deed so far
  That it becomes a virtue.

ISABELLA   O you beast!
  O faithless coward! O dishonest wretch!   140
  Wilt thou be made a man out of my vice?
  Is't not a kind of incest to take life
  From thine own sister's shame? What should I think?
  Heaven shield my mother played my father fair,
  For such a warpèd slip of wilderness
  Ne'er issued from his blood. Take my defiance,
  Die, perish. Might but my bending down
  Reprieve thee from thy fate, it should proceed.
  I'll pray a thousand prayers for thy death,
  No word to save thee.   150

CLAUDIO
  Nay, hear me, Isabel.

ISABELLA   O, fie, fie, fie!
  Thy sin's not accidental, but a trade.
  Mercy to thee would prove itself a bawd,
  'Tis best that thou diest quickly.   *Going*

CLAUDIO   O hear me, Isabella.

Duke comes forward

DUKE Vouchsafe a word, young sister, but one word.

ISABELLA What is your will?

DUKE Might you dispense with your leisure, I would by and by have some speech with you. The satisfaction I would require is likewise your own benefit.

160 ISABELLA I have no superfluous leisure. My stay must be stolen out of other affairs, but I will attend you a while.

DUKE (*aside*) Son, I have overheard what hath passed between you and your sister. Angelo had never the purpose to corrupt her; only he hath made an assay of her virtue to practise his judgement with the disposition of natures. She, having the truth of honour in her, hath made him that gracious denial which he is most glad to receive. I am confessor to Angelo, and I know this to be true. Therefore prepare yourself to death. Do not

170 satisfy your resolution with hopes that are fallible. Tomorrow you must die. Go to your knees and make ready.

CLAUDIO Let me ask my sister pardon. I am so out of love with life that I will sue to be rid of it.

DUKE Hold you there. Farewell.   *Exit Claudio*

Enter Provost

Provost, a word with you.

PROVOST What's your will, father?

DUKE That now you are come, you will be gone. Leave me a while with the maid. My mind promises with my

180 habit no loss shall touch her by my company.

PROVOST In good time.   *Exit*

DUKE The hand that hath made you fair hath made you good. The goodness that is cheap in beauty makes beauty brief in goodness, but grace, being the soul of your complexion, shall keep the body of it ever fair. The assault that Angelo hath made to you, fortune hath conveyed to my understanding, and, but that frailty hath examples for his falling, I should wonder at Angelo. How will you do to content this substitute, and to save your brother?   190

ISABELLA I am now going to resolve him. I had rather my brother die by the law than my son should be unlawfully born. But O, how much is the good Duke deceived in Angelo! If ever he return and I can speak to him, I will open my lips in vain, or discover his government.

DUKE That shall not be much amiss. Yet, as the matter now stands, he will avoid your accusation; he made trial of you only. Therefore fasten your ear on my advisings. To the love I have in doing good a remedy presents   200 itself. I do make myself believe that you may most uprighteously do a poor wronged lady a merited benefit, redeem your brother from the angry law, do no stain to your own gracious person, and much please the absent Duke, if peradventure he shall ever return to have hearing of this business.

ISABELLA Let me hear you speak farther. I have spirit to do anything that appears not foul in the truth of my spirit.

DUKE Virtue is bold, and goodness never fearful. Have   210 you not heard speak of Mariana, the sister of Frederick, the great soldier who miscarried at sea?

ISABELLA I have heard of the lady, and good words went with her name.

DUKE She should this Angelo have married, was affianced to her oath, and the nuptial appointed, between which time of the contract and limit of the solemnity, her brother Frederick was wrecked at sea, having in that perished vessel the dowry of his sister. But mark how heavily this befell to the poor gentlewoman. There she   220 lost a noble and renowned brother, in his love toward her ever most kind and natural; with him the portion and sinew of her fortune, her marriage dowry; with both, her combinate husband, this well-seeming Angelo.

ISABELLA Can this be so? Did Angelo so leave her?

DUKE Left her in her tears, and dried not one of them with his comfort, swallowed his vows whole, pretending in her discoveries of dishonour. In few, bestowed her on her own lamentation, which she yet wears for his sake, and he, a marble to her tears, is washed with them, but relents not.

ISABELLA What a merit were it in death to take this poor maid from the world! What corruption in this life, that it will let this man live! But how out of this can she avail?

DUKE It is a rupture that you may easily heal, and the cure of it not only saves your brother, but keeps you from dishonour in doing it.

ISABELLA Show me how, good father.

DUKE This forenamed maid hath yet in her the continuance of her first affection. His unjust unkindness, that in all reason should have quenched her love, hath, like an impediment in the current, made it more violent and unruly. Go you to Angelo, answer his requiring with a plausible obedience, agree with his demands to the point. Only refer yourself to this advantage: first, that your stay with him may not be long, that the time may have all shadow and silence in it, and the place answer to convenience. This being granted in course – and now follows all – we shall advise this wronged maid to stead up your appointment, go in your place. If the encounter acknowledge itself hereafter, it may compel him to her recompense, and here, by this is your brother saved, your honour untainted, the poor Mariana

advantaged, and the corrupt deputy scaled. The maid
will I frame and make fit for his attempt. If you think
well to carry this, as you may, the doubleness of the
benefit defends the deceit from reproof. What think you
of it?

ISABELLA The image of it gives me content already, and I   260
trust it will grow to a most prosperous perfection.

DUKE It lies much in your holding up. Haste you speedily
to Angelo. If for this night he entreat you to his bed,
give him promise of satisfaction. I will presently to
Saint Luke's. There, at the moated grange, resides this
dejected Mariana. At that place call upon me, and dispatch with Angelo, that it may be quickly.

ISABELLA I thank you for this comfort. Fare you well,
good father.   *Exit*

Enter Elbow, Pompey, and Officers   **III.2**

ELBOW Nay, if there be no remedy for it but that you will
needs buy and sell men and women like beasts, we shall
have all the world drink brown and white bastard.

DUKE O heavens, what stuff is here?

POMPEY 'Twas never merry world since, of two usuries,
the merriest was put down, and the worser allowed by
order of law a furred gown to keep him warm; and
furred with fox and lamb skins too, to signify that craft,
being richer than innocency, stands for the facing.

ELBOW Come your way, sir. Bless you, good father friar.   10

DUKE And you, good brother father. What offence hath
this man made you, sir?

ELBOW Marry, sir, he hath offended the law. And, sir, we
take him to be a thief too, sir, for we have found upon
him, sir, a strange picklock, which we have sent to the
deputy.

DUKE

    Fie, sirrah, a bawd, a wicked bawd!

    The evil that thou causest to be done,

    That is thy means to live. Do thou but think

20   What 'tis to cram a maw or clothe a back

    From such a filthy vice. Say to thyself,

    From their abominable and beastly touches

    I drink, I eat, array myself, and live.

    Canst thou believe thy living is a life,

    So stinkingly depending? Go mend, go mend.

POMPEY Indeed, it does stink in some sort, sir, but yet,
sir, I would prove —

DUKE

    Nay, if the devil have given thee proofs for sin,

    Thou wilt prove his. Take him to prison, officer.

30   Correction and instruction must both work

    Ere this rude beast will profit.

ELBOW He must before the deputy, sir. He has given him
warning. The deputy cannot abide a whoremaster. If he
be a whoremonger, and comes before him, he were as
good go a mile on his errand.

DUKE

    That we were all, as some would seem to be,

    Free from our faults, as faults from seeming free.

    Enter Lucio

ELBOW His neck will come to your waist — a cord, sir.

POMPEY I spy comfort, I cry bail. Here's a gentleman and

40 a friend of mine.

LUCIO How now, noble Pompey? What, at the wheels of
Caesar? Art thou led in triumph? What, is there none
of Pygmalion's images, newly made woman, to be had
now, for putting the hand in the pocket and extracting
it clutched? What reply? Ha? What say'st thou to this
tune, matter, and method? Is't not drowned i'th'last

rain, ha? What say'st thou, trot? Is the world as it was,
man? Which is the way? Is it sad, and few words?
Or how? The trick of it?

DUKE Still thus, and thus, still worse?   50

LUCIO How doth my dear morsel, thy mistress? Procures she still, ha?

POMPEY Troth, sir, she hath eaten up all her beef, and
she is herself in the tub.

LUCIO Why, 'tis good. It is the right of it. It must be so.
Ever your fresh whore and your powdered bawd. An
unshunned consequence, it must be so. Art going to
prison, Pompey?

POMPEY Yes, faith, sir.

LUCIO Why, 'tis not amiss, Pompey. Farewell. Go, say I   60
sent thee thither. For debt, Pompey? Or how?

ELBOW For being a bawd, for being a bawd.

LUCIO Well, then, imprison him. If imprisonment be the
due of a bawd, why, 'tis his right. Bawd is he doubtless,
and of antiquity too; bawd-born. Farewell, good
Pompey. Commend me to the prison, Pompey. You will
turn good husband now, Pompey. You will keep the
house.

POMPEY I hope, sir, your good worship will be my bail.

LUCIO No, indeed will I not, Pompey; it is not the wear. I 70
will pray, Pompey, to increase your bondage. If you
take it not patiently, why, your mettle is the more.
Adieu, trusty Pompey. Bless you, friar.

DUKE And you.

LUCIO Does Bridget paint still, Pompey, ha?

ELBOW Come your ways, sir, come.

POMPEY You will not bail me then, sir?

LUCIO Then, Pompey, nor now. What news abroad,
friar, what news?

ELBOW Come your ways, sir, come.   80

LUCIO Go to kennel, Pompey, go.

Exeunt Elbow, Pompey, and Officers

What news, friar, of the Duke?

DUKE I know none. Can you tell me of any?

LUCIO Some say he is with the Emperor of Russia; other some, he is in Rome. But where is he, think you?

DUKE I know not where, but wheresoever, I wish him well.

LUCIO It was a mad fantastical trick of him to steal from the state, and usurp the beggary he was never born to.
90 Lord Angelo dukes it well in his absence. He puts transgression to't.

DUKE He does well in't.

LUCIO A little more lenity to lechery would do no harm in him. Something too crabbed that way, friar.

DUKE It is too general a vice, and severity must cure it.

LUCIO Yes, in good sooth, the vice is of a great kindred. It is well allied, but it is impossible to extirp it quite, friar, till eating and drinking be put down. They say this Angelo was not made by man and woman after this
100 downright way of creation. Is it true, think you?

DUKE How should he be made, then?

LUCIO Some report a sea-maid spawned him. Some that he was begot between two stock-fishes. But it is certain that when he makes water his urine is congealed ice. That I know to be true. And he is a motion generative. That's infallible.

DUKE You are pleasant, sir, and speak apace.

LUCIO Why, what a ruthless thing is this in him, for the rebellion of a cod-piece to take away the life of a man!
110 Would the Duke that is absent have done this? Ere he would have hanged a man for the getting a hundred bastards, he would have paid for the nursing a thousand. He had some feeling of the sport. He knew the service,

and that instructed him to mercy.

DUKE I never heard the absent Duke much detected for
    women. He was not inclined that way.

LUCIO O, sir, you are deceived.

DUKE 'Tis not possible.

LUCIO Who? Not the Duke? Yes, your beggar of fifty,
    and his use was to put a ducat in her clack-dish. The   120
    Duke had crotchets in him. He would be drunk, too;
    that let me inform you.

DUKE You do him wrong, surely.

LUCIO Sir, I was an inward of his. A shy fellow was the
    Duke, and I believe I know the cause of his with-
    drawing.

DUKE What, I prithee, might be the cause?

LUCIO No, pardon. 'Tis a secret must be locked within
    the teeth and the lips. But this I can let you understand,
    the greater file of the subject held the Duke to be wise.   130

DUKE Wise? Why, no question but he was.

LUCIO A very superficial, ignorant, unweighing fellow.

DUKE Either this is envy in you, folly, or mistaking. The
    very stream of his life and the business he hath
    helmed must, upon a warranted need, give him a better
    proclamation. Let him be but testimonied in his own
    bringings-forth, and he shall appear to the envious a
    scholar, a statesman, and a soldier. Therefore you
    speak unskilfully; or, if your knowledge be more,
    it is much darkened in your malice.   140

LUCIO Sir, I know him, and I love him.

DUKE Love talks with better knowledge, and knowledge
    with dearer love.

LUCIO Come, sir, I know what I know.

DUKE I can hardly believe that, since you know not what
    you speak. But if ever the Duke return — as our prayers
    are he may — let me desire you to make your answer

before him. If it be honest you have spoke, you have
courage to maintain it. I am bound to call upon you, and,
150   I pray you, your name?

LUCIO Sir, my name is Lucio, well known to the Duke.

DUKE He shall know you better, sir, if I may live to report
you.

LUCIO I fear you not.

DUKE O, you hope the Duke will return no more, or you
imagine me too unhurtful an opposite. But indeed I can
do you little harm; you'll forswear this again.

LUCIO I'll be hanged first. Thou art deceived in me, friar.
But no more of this. Canst thou tell if Claudio die to-
160   morrow or no?

DUKE Why should he die, sir?

LUCIO Why? For filling a bottle with a tun-dish. I would
the Duke we talk of were returned again. This ungenitured agent will unpeople the province with con-
tinency. Sparrows must not build in his house-eaves
because they are lecherous. The Duke yet would have
dark deeds darkly answered. He would never bring
them to light. Would be were returned. Marry, this
Claudio is condemned for untrussing. Farewell, good
170   friar. I prithee, pray for me. The Duke, I say to thee
again, would eat mutton on Fridays. He's not past it
yet, and I say to thee, he would mouth with a beggar,
though she smelt brown bread and garlic. Say that I
said so. Farewell.   *Exit*

DUKE

No might nor greatness in mortality
Can censure 'scape; back-wounding calumny
The whitest virtue strikes. What king so strong
Can tie the gall up in the slanderous tongue?
But who comes here?

Enter Escalus, Provost, and Officers with Mistress
   Overdone

ESCALUS Go! Away with her to prison.   180

MISTRESS OVERDONE Good my lord, be good to me.
   Your honour is accounted a merciful man, good my
   lord.

ESCALUS Double and treble admonition, and still forfeit
   in the same kind? This would make mercy swear, and
   play the tyrant.

PROVOST A bawd of eleven years' continuance, may it
   please your honour.

MISTRESS OVERDONE My lord, this is one Lucio's
   information against me. Mistress Kate Keepdown was   190
   with child by him in the Duke's time. He promised her
   marriage. His child is a year and a quarter old, come
   Philip and Jacob. I have kept it myself, and see how he
   goes about to abuse me.

ESCALUS That fellow is a fellow of much licence. Let him
   be called before us. Away with her to prison. Go to, no
   more words. *Exeunt Officers with Mistress Overdone*
   Provost, my brother Angelo will not be altered. Claudio
   must die tomorrow. Let him be furnished with divines,
   and have all charitable preparation. If my brother   200
   wrought by my pity, it should not be so with him.

PROVOST So please you, this friar hath been with him,
   and advised him for th'entertainment of death.

ESCALUS Good even, good father.

DUKE Bliss and goodness on you!

ESCALUS Of whence are you?

DUKE
   Not of this country, though my chance is now
   To use it for my time. I am a brother
   Of gracious order, late come from the See,

210   In special business from his Holiness.

ESCALUS What news abroad i'th'world?

DUKE None, but that there is so great a fever on goodness that the dissolution of it must cure it. Novelty is only in request, and it is as dangerous to be aged in any kind of course as it is virtuous to be constant in any undertaking. There is scarce truth enough alive to make societies secure, but security enough to make fellowships accursed. Much upon this riddle runs the wisdom of the world. This news is old enough, yet it is every 220 day's news. I pray you, sir, of what disposition was the Duke?

ESCALUS One that, above all other strifes, contended especially to know himself.

DUKE What pleasure was he given to?

ESCALUS Rather rejoicing to see another merry than merry at anything which professed to make him rejoice: a gentleman of all temperance. But leave we him to his events, with a prayer they may prove prosperous, and let me desire to know how you find Claudio prepared. 230 I am made to understand that you have lent him visitation.

DUKE He professes to have received no sinister measure from his judge, but most willingly humbles himself to the determination of justice. Yet had he framed to himself, by the instruction of his frailty, many deceiving promises of life, which I, by my good leisure, have discredited to him, and now is he resolved to die.

ESCALUS You have paid the heavens your function, and the prisoner the very debt of your calling. I have 240 laboured for the poor gentleman to the extremest shore of my modesty, but my brother-justice have I found so severe that he hath forced me to tell him he is indeed Justice.

DUKE If his own life answer the straitness of his proceed-
ing, it shall become him well; wherein if he chance to
fail, he hath sentenced himself.

ESCALUS I am going to visit the prisoner. Fare you well.

DUKE Peace be with you!

Exeunt Escalus and Provost

He who the sword of heaven will bear
Should be as holy as severe;   250
Pattern in himself to know,
Grace to stand, and virtue go;
More nor less to others paying
Than by self-offences weighing.
Shame to him whose cruel striking
Kills for faults of his own liking.
Twice treble shame on Angelo,
To weed my vice and let his grow.
O, what may man within him hide,
Though angel on the outward side?   260
How may likeness made in crimes,
Making practice on the times,
To-draw with idle spiders' strings
Most ponderous and substantial things!
Craft against vice I must apply.
With Angelo tonight shall lie
His old betrothèd, but despised:
So disguise shall by th'disguised
Pay with falsehood, false exacting,
And perform an old contracting.   *Exit*   270

*

IV.I   *Enter Mariana, and Boy singing*

BOY (*sings*)

    Take, O take those lips away

       That so sweetly were forsworn;

    And those eyes, the break of day,

       Lights that do mislead the morn:

    But my kisses bring again, bring again;

    Seals of love, though sealed in vain, sealed in vain.

    Enter Duke as a friar

MARIANA

    Break off thy song, and haste thee quick away.

    Here comes a man of comfort, whose advice

    Hath often stilled my brawling discontent.   *Exit Boy*

10   I cry you mercy, sir, and well could wish

    You had not found me here so musical.

    Let me excuse me, and believe me so,

    My mirth it much displeased, but pleased my woe.

DUKE

    'Tis good, though music oft hath such a charm

    To make bad good, and good provoke to harm.

    I pray you tell me, hath anybody inquired for me here

    today? Much upon this time have I promised here to

    meet.

MARIANA You have not been inquired after. I have sat

20   here all day.

    Enter Isabella

DUKE I do constantly believe you. The time is come even

    now. I shall crave your forbearance a little. May be I

    will call upon you anon for some advantage to yourself.

MARIANA I am always bound to you.   *Exit*

DUKE

    Very well met, and welcome.

    What is the news from this good deputy?

ISABELLA

   He hath a garden circummured with brick,
   Whose western side is with a vineyard backed;
   And to that vineyard is a planchèd gate,
   That makes his opening with this bigger key.   30
   This other doth command a little door
   Which from the vineyard to the garden leads.
   There have I made my promise,
   Upon the heavy middle of the night,
   To call upon him.

DUKE

   But shall you on your knowledge find this way?

ISABELLA

   I have ta'en a due and wary note upon't.
   With whispering and most guilty diligence,
   In action all of precept, he did show me
   The way twice o'er.

DUKE   Are there no other tokens   40
   Between you 'greed concerning her observance?

ISABELLA

   No, none, but only a repair i'th'dark,
   And that I have possessed him my most stay
   Can be but brief. For I have made him know
   I have a servant comes with me along,
   That stays upon me, whose persuasion is
   I come about my brother.

DUKE   'Tis well borne up.
   I have not yet made known to Mariana
   A word of this. What ho, within. Come forth.
     Enter Mariana
   I pray you, be acquainted with this maid;   50
   She comes to do you good.

ISABELLA   I do desire the like.

DUKE

Do you persuade yourself that I respect you?

MARIANA

Good friar, I know you do, and so have found it.

DUKE

Take then this your companion by the hand,
Who hath a story ready for your ear.
I shall attend your leisure, but make haste.
The vaporous night approaches.

MARIANA

Will't please you walk aside?

Exeunt Mariana and Isabella

DUKE

O place and greatness, millions of false eyes
60   Are stuck upon thee. Volumes of report
Run with these false, and most contrarious quest
Upon thy doings; thousand escapes of wit
Make thee the father of their idle dream,
And rack thee in their fancies.

Enter Mariana and Isabella

                  Welcome, how agreed?

ISABELLA

She'll take the enterprise upon her, father,
If you advise it.

DUKE   It is not my consent,
But my entreaty too.

ISABELLA   Little have you to say
When you depart from him but, soft and low,
'Remember now my brother.'

MARIANA   Fear me not.

DUKE

70   Nor, gentle daughter, fear you not at all.
He is your husband on a pre-contract.

To bring you thus together, 'tis no sin,
Sith that the justice of your title to him
Doth flourish the deceit. Come, let us go;
Our corn's to reap, for yet our tithe's to sow. *Exeunt*

Enter Provost and Pompey   IV.2

PROVOST Come hither, sirrah. Can you cut off a man's head?

POMPEY If the man be a bachelor, sir, I can; but if he be a married man, he's his wife's head, and I can never cut off a woman's head.

PROVOST Come, sir, leave me your snatches, and yield me a direct answer. Tomorrow morning are to die Claudio and Barnardine. Here is in our prison a common executioner, who in his office lacks a helper. If you will take it on you to assist him, it shall redeem you 10 from your gyves; if not, you shall have your full time of imprisonment, and your deliverance with an unpitied whipping, for you have been a notorious bawd.

POMPEY Sir, I have been an unlawful bawd time out of mind, but yet I will be content to be a lawful hangman. I would be glad to receive some instruction from my fellow partner.

PROVOST What ho, Abhorson! Where's Abhorson, there?

Enter Abhorson

ABHORSON Do you call, sir?

PROVOST Sirrah, here's a fellow will help you tomorrow 20 in your execution. If you think it meet, compound with him by the year, and let him abide here with you; if not, use him for the present and dismiss him. He cannot plead his estimation with you. He hath been a bawd.

ABHORSON A bawd, sir? Fie upon him, he will discredit our mystery.

PROVOST Go to, sir, you weigh equally. A feather will
    turn the scale.   *Exit*

POMPEY Pray, sir, by your good favour – for surely, sir, a
30   good favour you have, but that you have a hanging
    look – do you call, sir, your occupation a mystery?

ABHORSON Ay, sir, a mystery.

POMPEY Painting, sir, I have heard say, is a mystery, and
    your whores, sir, being members of my occupation,
    using painting, do prove my occupation a mystery. But
    what mystery there should be in hanging, if I should be
    hanged, I cannot imagine.

ABHORSON Sir, it is a mystery.

POMPEY Proof?

40 ABHORSON Every true man's apparel fits your thief –

POMPEY If it be too little for your thief, your true man
    thinks it big enough. If it be too big for your thief, your
    thief thinks it little enough. So every true man's apparel
    fits your thief.

    Enter Provost

PROVOST Are you agreed?

POMPEY Sir, I will serve him, for I do find your hang-
    man is a more penitent trade than your bawd. He doth
    oftener ask forgiveness.

PROVOST You, sirrah, provide your block and your axe
50   tomorrow four o'clock.

ABHORSON Come, on, bawd. I will instruct thee in my
    trade. Follow!

POMPEY I do desire to learn, sir, and I hope, if you have
    occasion to use me for your own turn, you shall find me
    yare. For truly, sir, for your kindness I owe you a good
    turn.

PROVOST
    Call hither Barnardine and Claudio.

                         Exeunt Pompey and Abhorson

Th'one has my pity; not a jot the other,
Being a murderer, though he were my brother.
    Enter Claudio
Look, here's the warrant, Claudio, for thy death.   60
'Tis now dead midnight, and by eight tomorrow
Thou must be made immortal. Where's Barnardine?

CLAUDIO

As fast locked up in sleep as guiltless labour
When it lies starkly in the traveller's bones.
He will not wake.

PROVOST   Who can do good on him?
Well, go, prepare yourself.
    Knocking

                        But hark, what noise?
Heaven give your spirits comfort.   *Exit Claudio*
                        By and by.
I hope it is some pardon or reprieve
For the most gentle Claudio.
    Enter Duke as a friar

                        Welcome, father.

DUKE

The best and wholesom'st spirits of the night   70
Envelop you, good provost. Who called here of late?

PROVOST

None since the curfew rung.

DUKE

Not Isabel?

PROVOST   No.

DUKE   They will then, ere't be long.

PROVOST

What comfort is for Claudio?

DUKE

There's some in hope.

PROVOST   It is a bitter deputy.

DUKE

> Not so, not so; his life is paralleled
> Even with the stroke and line of his great justice.
> He doth with holy abstinence subdue
> That in himself which he spurs on his power
> To qualify in others. Were he mealed with that
> Which he corrects, then were he tyrannous,
> But this being so, he's just.

> > *Knocking*

> > > > Now are they come.

> > > > > *Exit Provost*

> This is a gentle provost; seldom when
> The steelèd gaoler is the friend of men.

> > *Knocking*

> How now? What noise? That spirit's possessed with
> > haste
> That wounds th'unsisting postern with these strokes.

> > *Enter Provost*

PROVOST

> There he must stay until the officer
> Arise to let him in. He is called up.

DUKE

> Have you no countermand for Claudio yet,
> But he must die tomorrow?

PROVOST   None, sir, none.

DUKE

> As near the dawning, provost, as it is,
> You shall hear more ere morning.

PROVOST   Happily

> You something know, yet I believe there comes
> No countermand; no such example have we.
> Besides, upon the very siege of justice,
> Lord Angelo hath to the public ear
> Professed the contrary.

80

90

Enter a Messenger

DUKE This is his lordship's man.

PROVOST And here comes Claudio's pardon.

MESSENGER My lord hath sent you this note, and by me   100
this further charge: that you swerve not from the smallest
article of it, neither in time, matter, or other circum-
stance. Good morrow; for, as I take it, it is almost day.

PROVOST I shall obey him.   *Exit Messenger*

DUKE (*aside*)

This is his pardon, purchased by such sin
For which the pardoner himself is in:
Hence hath offence his quick celerity,
When it is borne in high authority.
When vice makes mercy, mercy's so extended
That for the fault's love is th'offender friended.   110
Now, sir, what news?

PROVOST I told you. Lord Angelo, belike thinking me re-
miss in mine office, awakens me with this unwonted
putting on – methinks strangely, for he hath not used
it before.

DUKE Pray you, let's hear.

PROVOST (*reads the letter*) *Whatsoever you may hear to the
contrary, let Claudio be executed by four of the clock, and,
in the afternoon, Barnardine. For my better satisfaction,
let me have Claudio's head sent me by five. Let this be*   120
*duly performed, with a thought that more depends on it
than we must yet deliver. Thus fail not to do your office,
as you will answer it at your peril.*
What say you to this, sir?

DUKE What is that Barnardine who is to be executed in
th'afternoon?

PROVOST A Bohemian born, but here nursed up and
bred. One that is a prisoner nine years old.

DUKE How came it that the absent Duke had not either

130   delivered him to his liberty or executed him? I have
    heard it was ever his manner to do so.

PROVOST His friends still wrought reprieves for him;
    and, indeed, his fact, till now in the government of Lord
    Angelo, came not to an undoubtful proof.

DUKE It is now apparent?

PROVOST Most manifest, and not denied by himself.

DUKE Hath he borne himself penitently in prison? How
    seems he to be touched?

PROVOST A man that apprehends death no more dread-
140   fully but as a drunken sleep; careless, reckless, and
    fearless of what's past, present, or to come; insensible
    of mortality, and desperately mortal.

DUKE He wants advice.

PROVOST He will hear none. He hath evermore had the
    liberty of the prison. Give him leave to escape hence, he
    would not. Drunk many times a day, if not many days
    entirely drunk. We have very oft awaked him, as if to
    carry him to execution, and showed him a seeming
    warrant for it. It hath not moved him at all.

150 DUKE More of him anon. There is written in your brow,
    provost, honesty and constancy. If I read it not truly,
    my ancient skill beguiles me; but in the boldness of my
    cunning I will lay myself in hazard. Claudio, whom
    here you have warrant to execute, is no greater forfeit
    to the law than Angelo who hath sentenced him. To make
    you understand this in a manifested effect, I crave but
    four days' respite, for the which you are to do me both a
    present and a dangerous courtesy.

PROVOST Pray, sir, in what?

160 DUKE In the delaying death.

PROVOST Alack, how may I do it, having the hour limited,
    and an express command, under penalty, to deliver his
    head in the view of Angelo? I may make my case as

Claudio's, to cross this in the smallest.

DUKE By the vow of mine order I warrant you, if my instructions may be your guide. Let this Barnardine be this morning executed, and his head borne to Angelo.

PROVOST Angelo hath seen them both, and will discover the favour.

DUKE O, death's a great disguiser, and you may add to it. 170
Shave the head, and tie the beard, and say it was the desire of the penitent to be so bared before his death. You know the course is common. If anything fall to you upon this, more than thanks and good fortune, by the saint whom I profess, I will plead against it with my life.

PROVOST Pardon me, good father, it is against my oath.

DUKE Were you sworn to the Duke or to the deputy?

PROVOST To him, and to his substitutes.

DUKE You will think you have made no offence if the Duke avouch the justice of your dealing? 180

PROVOST But what likelihood is in that?

DUKE Not a resemblance, but a certainty. Yet since I see you fearful, that neither my coat, integrity, nor persuasion can with ease attempt you, I will go further than I meant, to pluck all fears out of you. Look you, sir, here is the hand and seal of the Duke. You know the character, I doubt not, and the signet is not strange to you.

PROVOST I know them both.

DUKE The contents of this is the return of the Duke. You 190
shall anon over-read it at your pleasure, where you shall find within these two days he will be here. This is a thing that Angelo knows not, for he this very day receives letters of strange tenor, perchance of the Duke's death, perchance entering into some monastery, but by chance nothing of what is writ. Look, th'unfolding star calls up the shepherd. Put not yourself into amazement

how these things should be. All difficulties are but easy
when they are known. Call your executioner, and off
200   with Barnardine's head. I will give him a present
shrift and advise him for a better place. Yet you are
amazed, but this shall absolutely resolve you. Come
away, it is almost clear dawn.   *Exit with Provost*

IV.3   *Enter Pompey*

POMPEY I am as well acquainted here as I was in our
house of profession. One would think it were Mistress
Overdone's own house, for here be many of her old
customers. First, here's young Master Rash. He's in for
a commodity of brown paper and old ginger, nine-score
and seventeen pounds, of which he made five marks
ready money. Marry, then ginger was not much in request, for the old women were all dead. Then is there
here one Master Caper, at the suit of Master Threepile
10   the mercer, for some four suits of peach-coloured satin,
which now peaches him a beggar. Then have we here
young Dizzy, and young Master Deepvow, and Master
Copperspur, and Master Starve-lackey, the rapier and
dagger man, and young Drop-heir that killed lusty
Pudding, and Master Forthright the tilter, and brave
Master Shoe-tie the great traveller, and wild Half-can
that stabbed Pots, and I think forty more, all great doers
in our trade, and are now 'for the Lord's sake'.

Enter Abhorson

ABHORSON Sirrah, bring Barnardine hither.

20   POMPEY Master Barnardine, you must rise and be
hanged, Master Barnardine.

ABHORSON What ho, Barnardine!

BARNARDINE (*within*) A pox o' your throats! Who makes
that noise there? What are you?

POMPEY Your friends, sir, the hangman. You must be so good, sir, to rise and be put to death.

BARNARDINE (*within*) Away, you rogue, away! I am sleepy.

ABHORSON Tell him he must awake, and that quickly too.

POMPEY Pray, Master Barnardine, awake till you are 30 executed, and sleep afterwards.

ABHORSON Go in to him, and fetch him out.

POMPEY He is coming, sir, he is coming. I hear his straw rustle.

    Enter Barnardine

ABHORSON Is the axe upon the block, sirrah?

POMPEY Very ready, sir.

BARNARDINE How now, Abhorson, what's the news with you?

ABHORSON Truly, sir, I would desire you to clap into your prayers, for look you, the warrant's come. 40

BARNARDINE You rogue, I have been drinking all night. I am not fitted for't.

POMPEY O, the better, sir, for he that drinks all night, and is hanged betimes in the morning, may sleep the sounder all the next day.

    Enter Duke as a friar

ABHORSON Look you, sir, here comes your ghostly father. Do we jest now, think you?

DUKE Sir, induced by my charity, and hearing how hastily you are to depart, I am come to advise you, comfort you, and pray with you. 50

BARNARDINE Friar, not I. I have been drinking hard all night and I will have more time to prepare me, or they shall beat out my brains with billets. I will not consent to die this day, that's certain.

DUKE O, sir, you must, and therefore I beseech you look forward on the journey you shall go.

BARNARDINE I swear I will not die today for any man's
    persuasion.

DUKE But hear you.

60 BARNARDINE Not a word. If you have anything to say to
    me, come to my ward, for thence will not I today. *Exit*
        Enter Provost

DUKE
    Unfit to live or die. O gravel heart!
    After him, fellows: bring him to the block.
                                Exeunt Abhorson and Pompey

PROVOST
    Now, sir, how do you find the prisoner?

DUKE
    A creature unprepared, unmeet for death,
    And to transport him in the mind he is
    Were damnable.

PROVOST   Here in the prison, father,
    There died this morning of a cruel fever
    One Ragozine, a most notorious pirate,
70 A man of Claudio's years, his beard and head
    Just of his colour. What if we do omit
    This reprobate till he were well inclined,
    And satisfy the deputy with the visage
    Of Ragozine, more like to Claudio?

DUKE
    O, 'tis an accident that heaven provides.
    Dispatch it presently; the hour draws on
    Prefixed by Angelo. See this be done,
    And sent according to command, whiles I
    Persuade this rude wretch willingly to die.

PROVOST
80 This shall be done, good father, presently,
    But Barnardine must die this afternoon,
    And how shall we continue Claudio,

To save me from the danger that might come
If he were known alive?

DUKE   Let this be done.
Put them in secret holds, both Barnardine
And Claudio. Ere twice the sun hath made
His journal greeting to yond generation,
You shall find your safety manifested.

PROVOST

I am your free dependant.

DUKE

Quick, dispatch, and send the head to Angelo.   90

Exit Provost

Now will I write letters to Angelo –
The provost, he shall bear them – whose contents
Shall witness to him I am near at home,
And that by great injunctions I am bound
To enter publicly. Him I'll desire
To meet me at the consecrated fount
A league below the city, and from thence,
By cold gradation and well-balanced form,
We shall proceed with Angelo.

Enter Provost

PROVOST

Here is the head. I'll carry it myself.   100

DUKE

Convenient is it. Make a swift return,
For I would commune with you of such things
That want no ear but yours.

PROVOST   I'll make all speed.   *Exit*

ISABELLA (*within*)

Peace, ho, be here.

DUKE

The tongue of Isabel. She's come to know
If yet her brother's pardon be come hither,

But I will keep her ignorant of her good,
To make her heavenly comforts of despair
When it is least expected.

Enter Isabella

ISABELLA   Ho, by your leave!
DUKE
110 Good morning to you, fair and gracious daughter.
ISABELLA
The better, given me by so holy a man.
Hath yet the deputy sent my brother's pardon?
DUKE
He hath released him, Isabel, from the world.
His head is off and sent to Angelo.
ISABELLA
Nay, but it is not so.
DUKE
It is no other. Show your wisdom, daughter,
In your close patience.
ISABELLA
O, I will to him and pluck out his eyes!
DUKE
You shall not be admitted to his sight.
ISABELLA
120 Unhappy Claudio! Wretched Isabel!
Injurious world! Most damnèd Angelo!
DUKE
This nor hurts him nor profits you a jot;
Forbear it therefore, give your cause to heaven.
Mark what I say, which you shall find
By every syllable a faithful verity.
The Duke comes home tomorrow – nay, dry your eyes –
One of our covent, and his confessor,
Gives me this instance. Already he hath carried
Notice to Escalus and Angelo,

Who do prepare to meet him at the gates,   130
There to give up their power. If you can, pace your
    wisdom
In that good path that I would wish it go,
And you shall have your bosom on this wretch,
Grace of the Duke, revenges to your heart,
And general honour.

ISABELLA   I am directed by you.

DUKE
This letter then to Friar Peter give.
'Tis that he sent me of the Duke's return.
Say, by this token, I desire his company
At Mariana's house tonight. Her cause and yours
I'll perfect him withal, and he shall bring you   140
Before the Duke; and to the head of Angelo
Accuse him home and home. For my poor self,
I am combinèd by a sacred vow
And shall be absent. Wend you with this letter.
Command these fretting waters from your eyes
With a light heart. Trust not my holy order
If I pervert your course. Who's here?

    Enter Lucio

LUCIO Good even. Friar, where's the provost?

DUKE Not within, sir.

LUCIO O pretty Isabella, I am pale at mine heart to see   150
thine eyes so red. Thou must be patient. I am fain to
dine and sup with water and bran. I dare not for my
head fill my belly; one fruitful meal would set me to't.
But they say the Duke will be here tomorrow. By my
troth, Isabel, I loved thy brother. If the old fantastical
Duke of dark corners had been at home, he had lived.

    Exit Isabella

DUKE Sir, the Duke is marvellous little beholding to your
reports, but the best is, he lives not in them.

LUCIO Friar, thou knowest not the Duke so well as I do.
160   He's a better woodman than thou tak'st him for.

DUKE Well, you'll answer this one day. Fare ye well.

LUCIO Nay, tarry, I'll go along with thee. I can tell thee
     pretty tales of the Duke.

DUKE You have told me too many of him already, sir, if
     they be true; if not true, none were enough.

LUCIO I was once before him for getting a wench with
     child.

DUKE Did you such a thing?

LUCIO Yes, marry, did I, but I was fain to forswear it.
170   They would else have married me to the rotten medlar.

DUKE Sir, your company is fairer than honest. Rest you
     well.

LUCIO By my troth, I'll go with thee to the lane's end. If
     bawdy talk offend you, we'll have very little of it. Nay,
     friar, I am a kind of burr, I shall stick.   *Exeunt*

IV.4   *Enter Angelo and Escalus*

ESCALUS Every letter he hath writ hath disvouched other.

ANGELO In most uneven and distracted manner. His
     actions show much like to madness. Pray heaven his
     wisdom be not tainted. And why meet him at the gates,
     and reliver our authorities there?

ESCALUS I guess not.

ANGELO And why should we proclaim it in an hour before
     his entering, that if any crave redress of injustice, they
     should exhibit their petitions in the street?

10 ESCALUS He shows his reason for that – to have a dispatch
     of complaints, and to deliver us from devices hereafter,
     which shall then have no power to stand against us.

ANGELO
     Well, I beseech you let it be proclaimed.

Betimes i'th'morn I'll call you at your house.
Give notice to such men of sort and suit
As are to meet him.

ESCALUS   I shall, sir. Fare you well.

ANGELO
Good night.   *Exit Escalus*
This deed unshapes me quite, makes me unpregnant
And dull to all proceedings. A deflowered maid,
And by an eminent body that enforced   20
The law against it! But that her tender shame
Will not proclaim against her maiden loss,
How might she tongue me? Yet reason dares her no,
For my authority bears so credent bulk
That no particular scandal once can touch
But it confounds the breather. He should have lived,
Save that his riotous youth with dangerous sense
Might in the times to come have ta'en revenge,
By so receiving a dishonoured life
With ransom of such shame. Would yet he had lived.   30
Alack, when once our grace we have forgot,
Nothing goes right. We would, and we would not.
                                     Exit

Enter Duke, in his own habit, and Friar Peter   IV.5

DUKE
These letters at fit time deliver me.
The provost knows our purpose and our plot.
The matter being afoot, keep your instruction,
And hold you ever to our special drift,
Though sometimes you do blench from this to that,
As cause doth minister. Go call at Flavius' house,
And tell him where I stay. Give the like notice
To Valentius, Rowland, and to Crassus,

And bid them bring the trumpets to the gate;
10   But send me Flavius first.

FRIAR PETER   It shall be speeded well.

Exit

    Enter Varrius

DUKE
I thank thee, Varrius, thou hast made good haste.
Come, we will walk. There's other of our friends
Will greet us here anon, my gentle Varrius.   *Exeunt*

IV.6   *Enter Isabella and Mariana*

ISABELLA
To speak so indirectly I am loath.
I would say the truth, but to accuse him so,
That is your part. Yet I am advised to do it,
He says, to veil full purpose.

MARIANA   Be ruled by him.

ISABELLA
Besides, he tells me that if peradventure
He speak against me on the adverse side,
I should not think it strange, for 'tis a physic
That's bitter to sweet end.

MARIANA
I would Friar Peter –

    Enter Friar Peter

ISABELLA   O, peace, the friar is come.

FRIAR PETER
10   Come, I have found you out a stand most fit,
Where you may have such vantage on the Duke
He shall not pass you. Twice have the trumpets
    sounded.
The generous and gravest citizens

Have hent the gates, and very near upon
The Duke is entering. Therefore hence, away. *Exeunt*

*

Enter Duke, Varrius, Lords, Angelo, Escalus, Lucio,   **V.1**
Provost, Officers, and Citizens at several doors

DUKE

My very worthy cousin, fairly met.
Our old and faithful friend, we are glad to see you.

ANGELO *and* ESCALUS

Happy return be to your royal grace.

DUKE

Many and hearty thankings to you both.
We have made inquiry of you, and we hear
Such goodness of your justice that our soul
Cannot but yield you forth to public thanks,
Forerunning more requital.

ANGELO   You make my bonds still greater.

DUKE

O, your desert speaks loud, and I should wrong it
To lock it in the wards of covert bosom,   10
When it deserves with characters of brass
A forted residence 'gainst the tooth of time
And razure of oblivion. Give we our hand,
And let the subject see, to make them know
That outward courtesies would fain proclaim
Favours that keep within. Come, Escalus,
You must walk by us on our other hand,
And good supporters are you.

Enter Friar Peter and Isabella

FRIAR PETER

Now is your time. Speak loud and kneel before him.

ISABELLA

20   Justice, O royal Duke! Vail your regard
        Upon a wronged – I would fain have said, a maid.
        O worthy prince, dishonour not your eye
        By throwing it on any other object
        Till you have heard me in my true complaint
        And given me justice, justice, justice, justice!

DUKE

        Relate your wrongs. In what? By whom? Be brief.
        Here is Lord Angelo shall give you justice.
        Reveal yourself to him.

ISABELLA   O worthy Duke,
        You bid me seek redemption of the devil.

30   Hear me yourself, for that which I must speak
        Must either punish me, not being believed,
        Or wring redress from you. Hear me, O hear me, hear.

ANGELO

        My lord, her wits, I fear me, are not firm.
        She hath been a suitor to me for her brother,
        Cut off by course of justice –

ISABELLA   By course of justice!

ANGELO

        And she will speak most bitterly and strange.

ISABELLA

        Most strange, but yet most truly, will I speak.
        That Angelo's forsworn, is it not strange?
        That Angelo's a murderer, is't not strange?

40   That Angelo is an adulterous thief,
        An hypocrite, a virgin-violator,
        Is it not strange, and strange?

DUKE   Nay, it is ten times strange.

ISABELLA

        It is not truer he is Angelo
        Than this is all as true as it is strange.

Nay, it is ten times true, for truth is truth
To th'end of reck'ning.

DUKE   Away with her. Poor soul,
She speaks this in th'infirmity of sense.

ISABELLA
O prince, I conjure thee, as thou believ'st
There is another comfort than this world,
That thou neglect me not with that opinion   50
That I am touched with madness. Make not impossible
That which but seems unlike. 'Tis not impossible
But one, the wicked'st caitiff on the ground,
May seem as shy, as grave, as just, as absolute
As Angelo. Even so may Angelo,
In all his dressings, characts, titles, forms,
Be an arch-villain. Believe it, royal prince.
If he be less, he's nothing: but he's more,
Had I more name for badness.

DUKE   By mine honesty,
If she be mad, as I believe no other,   60
Her madness hath the oddest frame of sense,
Such a dependency of thing on thing,
As e'er I heard in madness.

ISABELLA   O gracious Duke,
Harp not on that, nor do not banish reason
For inequality, but let your reason serve
To make the truth appear where it seems hid,
And hide the false seems true.

DUKE   Many that are not mad
Have sure more lack of reason. What would you say?

ISABELLA
I am the sister of one Claudio,
Condemned upon the act of fornication   70
To lose his head, condemned by Angelo.
I, in probation of a sisterhood,

Was sent to by my brother. One Lucio
As then the messenger –

LUCIO   That's I, an't like your grace.
I came to her from Claudio, and desired her
To try her gracious fortune with Lord Angelo
For her poor brother's pardon.

ISABELLA   That's he indeed.

DUKE
You were not bid to speak.

LUCIO   No, my good lord,
Nor wished to hold my peace.

DUKE   I wish you now, then.
80   Pray you, take note of it, and when you have
A business for yourself, pray heaven you then
Be perfect.

LUCIO   I warrant your honour.

DUKE
The warrant's for yourself: take heed to't.

ISABELLA
This gentleman told somewhat of my tale.

LUCIO
Right.

DUKE
It may be right, but you are i'the wrong
To speak before your time. Proceed.

ISABELLA   I went
To this pernicious caitiff deputy –

DUKE
That's somewhat madly spoken.

ISABELLA   Pardon it,
90   The phrase is to the matter.

DUKE
Mended again. The matter. Proceed.

ISABELLA

In brief, to set the needless process by,
How I persuaded, how I prayed, and kneeled,
How he refelled me, and how I replied –
For this was of much length – the vile conclusion
I now begin with grief and shame to utter.
He would not, but by gift of my chaste body
To his concup'scible intemperate lust,
Release my brother, and after much debatement
My sisterly remorse confutes mine honour,   100
And I did yield to him. But the next morn betimes,
His purpose surfeiting, he sends a warrant
For my poor brother's head.

DUKE   This is most likely!

ISABELLA

O, that it were as like as it is true.

DUKE

By heaven, fond wretch, thou know'st not what thou
        speak'st,
Or else thou art suborned against his honour
In hateful practice. First, his integrity
Stands without blemish. Next, it imports no reason
That with such vehemency he should pursue
Faults proper to himself. If he had so offended,   110
He would have weighed thy brother by himself,
And not have cut him off. Someone hath set you on.
Confess the truth, and say by whose advice
Thou cam'st here to complain.

ISABELLA   And is this all?

Then, O you blessèd ministers above,
Keep me in patience, and with ripened time
Unfold the evil which is here wrapped up
In countenance. Heaven shield your grace from woe,
As I thus wrongèd hence unbelievèd go.

DUKE

120   I know you'd fain be gone. An officer!
    To prison with her. Shall we thus permit
    A blasting and a scandalous breath to fall
    On him so near us? This needs must be a practice.
    Who knew of your intent and coming hither?

ISABELLA

    One that I would were here, Friar Lodowick.

DUKE

    A ghostly father, belike. Who knows that Lodowick?

LUCIO

    My lord, I know him, 'tis a meddling friar;
    I do not like the man. Had he been lay, my lord,
    For certain words he spake against your grace
130   In your retirement I had swinged him soundly.

DUKE

    Words against me? This' a good friar, belike,
    And to set on this wretched woman here
    Against our substitute! Let this friar be found.

LUCIO

    But yesternight, my lord, she and that friar,
    I saw them at the prison. A saucy friar,
    A very scurvy fellow.

FRIAR PETER

    Blessed be your royal grace,
    I have stood by, my lord, and I have heard
    Your royal ear abused. First hath this woman
140   Most wrongfully accused your substitute,
    Who is as free from touch or soil with her
    As she from one ungot.

DUKE   We did believe no less.
    Know you that Friar Lodowick that she speaks of?

FRIAR PETER

    I know him for a man divine and holy,

Not scurvy, nor a temporary meddler,
As he's reported by this gentleman,
And, on my trust, a man that never yet
Did – as he vouches – misreport your grace.

LUCIO

My lord, most villainously, believe it.

FRIAR PETER

Well, he in time may come to clear himself,   150
But at this instant he is sick, my lord,
Of a strange fever. Upon his mere request,
Being come to knowledge that there was complaint
Intended 'gainst Lord Angelo, came I hither,
To speak, as from his mouth, what he doth know
Is true and false, and what he with his oath
And all probation will make up full clear,
Whensoever he's convented. First, for this woman,
To justify this worthy nobleman,
So vulgarly and personally accused,   160
Her shall you hear disprovèd to her eyes,
Till she herself confess it.

DUKE   Good friar, let's hear it.
                           Isabella is led off, guarded

      Enter Mariana

Do you not smile at this, Lord Angelo?
O heaven, the vanity of wretched fools!
Give us some seats. Come, cousin Angelo,
In this I'll be impartial. Be you judge
Of your own cause. Is this the witness, friar?
First, let her show her face, and after speak.

MARIANA

Pardon, my lord, I will not show my face
Until my husband bid me.   170

DUKE What, are you married?

MARIANA No, my lord.

DUKE Are you a maid?

MARIANA No, my lord.

DUKE A widow, then?

MARIANA Neither, my lord.

DUKE Why, you are nothing then. Neither maid, widow,
nor wife?

LUCIO My lord, she may be a punk. For many of them are
180   neither maid, widow, nor wife.

DUKE
Silence that fellow. I would he had some cause
To prattle for himself.

LUCIO Well, my lord.

MARIANA
My lord, I do confess I ne'er was married,
And I confess besides I am no maid;
I have known my husband, yet my husband
Knows not that ever he knew me.

LUCIO He was drunk, then, my lord. It can be no better.

DUKE For the benefit of silence, would thou wert so too.

190 LUCIO Well, my lord.

DUKE
This is no witness for Lord Angelo.

MARIANA
Now I come to't, my lord:
She that accuses him of fornication
In selfsame manner doth accuse my husband;
And charges him, my lord, with such a time
When, I'll depose, I had him in mine arms,
With all th'effect of love.

ANGELO
Charges she more than me?

MARIANA   Not that I know.

DUKE
No? You say your husband?

MARIANA

    Why, just, my lord, and that is Angelo,   200
    Who thinks he knows that he ne'er knew my body,
    But knows, he thinks, that he knows Isabel's.

ANGELO

    This is a strange abuse. Let's see thy face.

MARIANA

    My husband bids me. Now I will unmask.
       She unveils
    This is that face, thou cruel Angelo,
    Which once thou swor'st was worth the looking on.
    This is the hand which, with a vowed contract,
    Was fast belocked in thine. This is the body
    That took away the match from Isabel,
    And did supply thee at thy garden-house   210
    In her imagined person.

DUKE   Know you this woman?

LUCIO

    Carnally, she says.

DUKE   Sirrah, no more!

LUCIO

    Enough, my lord.

ANGELO

    My lord, I must confess I know this woman,
    And five years since there was some speech of marriage
    Betwixt myself and her, which was broke off,
    Partly for that her promisèd proportions
    Came short of composition, but in chief
    For that her reputation was disvalued
    In levity; since which time of five years   220
    I never spake with her, saw her, nor heard from her,
    Upon my faith and honour.

MARIANA   Noble prince,

As there comes light from heaven and words from
    breath,
As there is sense in truth and truth in virtue,
I am affianced this man's wife as strongly
As words could make up vows, and, my good lord,
But Tuesday night last gone in's garden-house
He knew me as a wife. As this is true,
Let me in safety raise me from my knees
Or else forever be confixèd here
A marble monument.

ANGELO   I did but smile till now.
Now, good my lord, give me the scope of justice.
My patience here is touched. I do perceive
These poor informal women are no more
But instruments of some more mightier member
That sets them on. Let me have way, my lord,
To find this practice out.

DUKE   Ay, with my heart,
And punish them to your height of pleasure.
Thou foolish friar, and thou pernicious woman,
Compact with her that's gone, think'st thou thy oaths,
Though they would swear down each particular saint,
Were testimonies against his worth and credit
That's sealed in approbation? You, Lord Escalus,
Sit with my cousin, lend him your kind pains
To find out this abuse, whence 'tis derived.
There is another friar that set them on;
Let him be sent for.

FRIAR PETER
Would he were here, my lord, for he indeed
Hath set the women on to this complaint.
Your provost knows the place where he abides
And he may fetch him.

DUKE   Go do it instantly;

Exit Provost

And you, my noble and well-warranted cousin,
Whom it concerns to hear this matter forth,
Do with your injuries as seems you best,
In any chastisement. I for a while
Will leave you; but stir not you till you have
Well determined upon these slanderers.

ESCALUS

My lord, we'll do it throughly.   *Exit Duke*
Signor Lucio, did not you say you knew that Friar
Lodowick to be a dishonest person?   260

LUCIO *Cucullus non facit monachum.* Honest in nothing
but in his clothes, and one that hath spoke most vil-
lainous speeches of the Duke.

ESCALUS We shall entreat you to abide here till he come
and enforce them against him. We shall find this friar a
notable fellow.

LUCIO As any in Vienna, on my word.

ESCALUS Call that same Isabel here once again. I would
speak with her.   *Exit an Attendant*
Pray you, my lord, give me leave to question. You shall   270
see how I'll handle her.

LUCIO Not better than he, by her own report.

ESCALUS Say you?

LUCIO Marry, sir, I think, if you handled her privately,
she would sooner confess. Perchance publicly she'll be
ashamed.

Enter Duke, as a friar, Provost, Isabella, and
Officers

ESCALUS I will go darkly to work with her.

LUCIO That's the way, for women are light at midnight.

ESCALUS Come on, mistress, here's a gentlewoman
denies all that you have said.   280

LUCIO My lord, here comes the rascal I spoke of — here
    with the provost.

ESCALUS In very good time. Speak not you to him, till we
    call upon you.

LUCIO Mum.

ESCALUS Come, sir, did you set these women on to
    slander Lord Angelo? They have confessed you did.

DUKE 'Tis false.

ESCALUS How? Know you where you are?

DUKE

290   Respect to your great place, and let the devil
    Be sometime honoured for his burning throne.
    Where is the Duke? 'Tis he should hear me speak.

ESCALUS

    The Duke's in us, and we will hear you speak.
    Look you speak justly.

DUKE

    Boldly at least. But O, poor souls,
    Come you to seek the lamb here of the fox?
    Good night to your redress. Is the Duke gone?
    Then is your cause gone too. The Duke's unjust,
    Thus to retort your manifest appeal
300   And put your trial in the villain's mouth
    Which here you come to accuse.

LUCIO

    This is the rascal. This is he I spoke of.

ESCALUS

    Why, thou unreverend and unhallowed friar,
    Is't not enough thou hast suborned these women
    To accuse this worthy man but, in foul mouth,
    And in the witness of his proper ear,
    To call him villain? And then to glance from him
    To th'Duke himself, to tax him with injustice?
    Take him hence. To th'rack with him. We'll touse you

Joint by joint, but we will know his purpose.   310
What? Unjust?

DUKE   Be not so hot. The Duke
Dare no more stretch this finger of mine than he
Dare rack his own. His subject am I not,
Nor here provincial. My business in this state
Made me a looker-on here in Vienna,
Where I have seen corruption boil and bubble
Till it o'errun the stew. Laws for all faults,
But faults so countenanced that the strong statutes
Stand like the forfeits in a barber's shop,
As much in mock as mark.   320

ESCALUS
Slander to th'state. Away with him to prison.

ANGELO
What can you vouch against him, Signor Lucio?
Is this the man that you did tell us of?

LUCIO 'Tis he, my lord. Come hither, goodman baldpate.
Do you know me?

DUKE I remember you, sir, by the sound of your voice. I
met you at the prison in the absence of the Duke.

LUCIO O, did you so? And do you remember what you
said of the Duke?

DUKE Most notedly, sir.   330

LUCIO Do you so, sir? And was the Duke a fleshmonger, a
fool, and a coward, as you then reported him to be?

DUKE You must, sir, change persons with me, ere you
make that my report. You, indeed, spoke so of him, and
much more, much worse.

LUCIO O thou damnable fellow, did not I pluck thee by
the nose for thy speeches?

DUKE I protest I love the Duke as I love myself.

ANGELO Hark how the villain would close now, after his
treasonable abuses.   340

ESCALUS Such a fellow is not to be talked withal. Away
with him to prison. Where is the provost? Away with
him to prison. Lay bolts enough upon him. Let him
speak no more. Away with those giglots too, and with
the other confederate companion.

The Provost lays hands on the Duke

DUKE Stay, sir, stay a while.

ANGELO What, resists he? Help him, Lucio.

LUCIO Come, sir, come, sir, come, sir! Foh, sir! Why, you
bald-pated, lying rascal, you must be hooded, must you?
350 Show your knave's visage, with a pox to you. Show
your sheep-biting face, and be hanged an hour. Will't
not off?

He pulls off the Friar's hood, and discovers the Duke

DUKE
Thou art the first knave that e'er mad'st a duke.
First, provost, let me bail these gentle three –
(*to Lucio*) Sneak not away, sir, for the friar and you
Must have a word anon. Lay hold on him.

LUCIO
This may prove worse than hanging.

DUKE (*to Escalus*)
What you have spoke I pardon. Sit you down.
We'll borrow place of him. (*To Angelo*) Sir, by your
leave.
360 Hast thou or word, or wit, or impudence
That yet can do thee office? If thou hast,
Rely upon it till my tale be heard,
And hold no longer out.

ANGELO   O my dread lord,
I should be guiltier than my guiltiness
To think I can be undiscernible,
When I perceive your grace, like power divine,
Hath looked upon my passes. Then, good prince,

No longer session hold upon my shame,
But let my trial be mine own confession.
Immediate sentence, then, and sequent death   370
Is all the grace I beg.

DUKE   Come hither, Mariana.
Say, wast thou e'er contracted to this woman?

ANGELO
I was, my lord.

DUKE
Go take her hence, and marry her instantly.
Do you the office, friar, which consummate,
Return him here again. Go with him, provost.
    Exit Angelo, with Mariana, Friar Peter, and Provost

ESCALUS
My lord, I am more amazed at his dishonour
Than at the strangeness of it.

DUKE   Come hither, Isabel.
Your friar is now your prince. As I was then
Advertising and holy to your business,   380
Not changing heart with habit, I am still
Attorneyed at your service.

ISABELLA   O, give me pardon,
That I, your vassal, have employed and pained
Your unknown sovereignty.

DUKE   You are pardoned, Isabel.
And now, dear maid, be you as free to us.
Your brother's death, I know, sits at your heart,
And you may marvel why I obscured myself,
Labouring to save his life, and would not rather
Make rash remonstrance of my hidden power
Than let him so be lost. O most kind maid,   390
It was the swift celerity of his death,
Which I did think with slower foot came on,
That brained my purpose; but peace be with him.

That life is better life past fearing death
'Than that which lives to fear. Make it your comfort,
So happy is your brother.

    Enter Angelo, Mariana, Friar Peter, Provost

ISABELLA   I do, my lord.

DUKE

For this new-married man approaching here,
Whose salt imagination yet hath wronged
Your well-defended honour, you must pardon
For Mariana's sake, but as he adjudged your brother,
Being criminal, in double violation
Of sacred chastity, and of promise-breach,
Thereon dependent, for your brother's life,
The very mercy of the law cries out
Most audible, even from his proper tongue,
'An Angelo for Claudio, death for death!'
Haste still pays haste, and leisure answers leisure,
Like doth quit like, and Measure still for Measure.
Then, Angelo, thy fault's thus manifested,
Which, though thou wouldst deny, denies thee vantage,
We do condemn thee to the very block
Where Claudio stooped to death, and with like haste.
Away with him.

MARIANA   O, my most gracious lord,
I hope you will not mock me with a husband.

DUKE

It is your husband mocked you with a husband.
Consenting to the safeguard of your honour
I thought your marriage fit; else imputation,
For that he knew you, might reproach your life
And choke your good to come. For his possessions,
Although by confiscation they are ours,
We do instate and widow you with all,
To buy you a better husband.

MARIANA   O my dear lord,
  I crave no other, nor no better man.

DUKE
  Never crave him. We are definitive.

MARIANA
  Gentle my liege! –

DUKE   You do but lose your labour.
  Away with him to death. (*To Lucio*) Now, sir, to you.

MARIANA
  O my good lord! Sweet Isabel, take my part,
  Lend me your knees, and, all my life to come,
  I'll lend you all my life to do you service.

DUKE
  Against all sense you do importune her.   430
  Should she kneel down in mercy of this fact,
  Her brother's ghost his pavèd bed would break,
  And take her hence in horror.

MARIANA   Isabel,
  Sweet Isabel, do yet but kneel by me.
  Hold up your hands, say nothing, I'll speak all.
  They say best men are moulded out of faults,
  And, for the most, become much more the better
  For being a little bad. So may my husband.
  O Isabel, will you not lend a knee?

DUKE
  He dies for Claudio's death.

ISABELLA (*kneeling*)   Most bounteous sir,   440
  Look, if it please you, on this man condemned
  As if my brother lived. I partly think
  A due sincerity governed his deeds
  Till he did look on me. Since it is so,
  Let him not die. My brother had but justice,
  In that he did the thing for which he died.
  For Angelo,

His act did not o'ertake his bad intent,
And must be buried but as an intent
450 That perished by the way. Thoughts are no subjects,
Intents but merely thoughts.

MARIANA   Merely, my lord.

DUKE

Your suit's unprofitable. Stand up, I say.
I have bethought me of another fault.
Provost, how came it Claudio was beheaded
At an unusual hour?

PROVOST   It was commanded so.

DUKE

Had you a special warrant for the deed?

PROVOST

No, my good lord, it was by private message.

DUKE

For which I do discharge you of your office;
Give up your keys.

PROVOST   Pardon me, noble lord,
460 I thought it was a fault, but knew it not,
Yet did repent me after more advice,
For testimony whereof, one in the prison
That should by private order else have died
I have reserved alive.

DUKE   What's he?

PROVOST   His name is Barnardine.

DUKE

I would thou hadst done so by Claudio.
Go, fetch him hither. Let me look upon him.

Exit Provost

ESCALUS

I am sorry one so learned and so wise
As you, Lord Angelo, have still appeared,
Should slip so grossly, both in the heat of blood

And lack of tempered judgement afterward.   470

ANGELO

I am sorry that such sorrow I procure,
And so deep sticks it in my penitent heart
That I crave death more willingly than mercy.
'Tis my deserving, and I do entreat it.

Enter Barnardine and Provost, Claudio muffled, and
Juliet

DUKE

Which is that Barnardine?

PROVOST   This, my lord.

DUKE

There was a friar told me of this man.
Sirrah, thou art said to have a stubborn soul,
That apprehends no further than this world,
And squar'st thy life according. Thou'rt condemned,
But, for those earthly faults, I quit them all,   480
And pray thee take this mercy to provide
For better times to come. Friar, advise him:
I leave him to your hand. What muffled fellow's that?

PROVOST

This is another prisoner that I saved,
Who should have died when Claudio lost his head,
As like almost to Claudio as himself.

He unmuffles Claudio

DUKE (*to Isabella*)

If he be like your brother, for his sake
Is he pardoned, and for your lovely sake,
Give me your hand and say you will be mine.
He is my brother too. But fitter time for that.   490
By this Lord Angelo perceives he's safe;
Methinks I see a quickening in his eye.
Well, Angelo, your evil quits you well.
Look that you love your wife, her worth worth yours.

I find an apt remission in myself,
And yet here's one in place I cannot pardon.
(*To Lucio*) You, sirrah, that knew me for a fool, a coward,
One all of luxury, an ass, a madman,
Wherein have I so deserved of you,
500   That you extol me thus?

LUCIO 'Faith, my lord, I spoke it but according to the
trick. If you will hang me for it, you may. But I had
rather it would please you I might be whipped.

DUKE

Whipped first, sir, and hanged after.
Proclaim it, provost, round about the city,
If any woman wronged by this lewd fellow –
As I have heard him swear himself there's one
Whom he begot with child – let her appear,
And he shall marry her. The nuptial finished,
510   Let him be whipped and hanged.

LUCIO I beseech your highness, do not marry me to a
whore. Your highness said even now, I made you a
duke. Good my lord, do not recompense me in making
me a cuckold.

DUKE

Upon mine honour, thou shalt marry her.
Thy slanders I forgive, and therewithal
Remit thy other forfeits. Take him to prison,
And see our pleasure herein executed.

LUCIO Marrying a punk, my lord, is pressing to death,
520   whipping, and hanging.

DUKE

Slandering a prince deserves it.

Exeunt Officers with Lucio

She, Claudio, that you wronged, look you restore.
Joy to you, Mariana. Love her, Angelo.
I have confessed her and I know her virtue.

Thanks, good friend Escalus, for thy much goodness.
There's more behind that is more gratulate.
Thanks, provost, for thy care and secrecy.
We shall employ thee in a worthier place.
Forgive him, Angelo, that brought you home
The head of Ragozine for Claudio's.   530
Th'offence pardons itself. Dear Isabel,
I have a motion much imports your good,
Whereto if you'll a willing ear incline,
What's mine is yours, and what is yours is mine.
So, bring us to our palace, where we'll show
What's yet behind, that's meet you all should know.

Exeunt

An Account of the Text
of this Edition

Measure for Measure was first printed in the Shakespeare Folio of 1623 (F). No antecedent quarto edition exists of the play. In the Folio edition, *Measure for Measure* stands fourth in the opening section of Comedies. The first five plays in F were set from copy especially prepared by Ralph Crane, a professional scrivener who is known to have done a great deal of work for the King's Men, Shakespeare's company. In 1621, when work on the Folio began at the printing-house of William Jaggard, probably four compositors of varying reliability set up the play from Crane's transcript which, while exemplary in its neatness and legibility, was also subject to the peculiarities and occasional inaccuracies identifiable in other Crane manuscripts that have survived. In fairness to Crane, it must be conceded that his task may not have been an easy one. There is ample evidence to show that his transcript was not based on the theatre prompt book, but rather on Shakespeare's so-called 'foul papers', which in this instance may be imagined as an untidy, and probably unrevised, draft which, stored away for close to two decades by the company, would have suffered a measure of deterioration (for the possibility that the text was later revised, perhaps by Thomas Middleton, see John Jowett and Gary Taylor, *Shakespeare Reshaped, 1606–23* (1993)).

It has become a commonplace for editors of *Measure for Measure* to quote Dr Johnson's judgement that 'there is perhaps not one of Shakespeare's plays more darkened than this by the peculiarities of its author, and the unskilfulness of its editors, by distortions of phrase, or negligence of transcription.' To be sure, the editorial tradition may at times have been less than skilful, and have incurred and perpetuated error; nor can the play be denied Shakespearian peculiarities. But Dr Johnson's sense that these darken the play may have more to do with his eighteenth-century sensibilities and approach to language and stylistic decorum than with what we now regard as standard Elizabethan English, or as Shakespeare's verbal and dramatic practices. The entire discipline of Shakespearian editing was put on a significantly new footing towards the end of the twentieth century, and one result of that has been the 'unediting' of Shakespeare, and the restoration of the text as it existed before Dr Johnson and his predecessors adjusted it to bring it into line with the stricter expectations of their day.

The present volume in the Penguin Shakespeare series is still based on the edition that J. M. Nosworthy edited and prepared for publication in 1969, but it also responds to more recent developments in Shakespearian textual scholarship. The text here provided is still basically Nosworthy's, and we shall still agree with him that the Folio printing of *Measure for Measure* provides some extraordinarily puzzling textual cruxes (for example, those at III.1.97, 100); arguably, in terms of editorial procedure, certain unintelligible readings should be allowed to stand, if only because no more persuasive alternatives have yet suggested themselves. With regard to the conservatism that Nosworthy claimed for his 1969 edition, the present reissue could be regarded as substantially more conservative than his (even though, from another point of view, it could be considered more radical). In particular, it un-edits a significant number of emendations that Nosworthy's text either inherited from the editorial tradition or was the first to introduce, and in their place restores the Folio text. At times, this can have significant consequences for the interpretation of the text (as at II.3.30–34). On the other hand, this edition also offers one new emendation of its own (at I.2.172). In a number of instances, the restoration of the Folio text has also involved omitting or adjusting passages of Nosworthy's commentary, while other notes have been altered to conform with the present Introduction.

JMN (1969), JRB (2005)

COLLATIONS

l

The selective list of collations which follows attempts to indicate all significant deviations from the F text. Readings which appear to be peculiar to the present edition are marked '*this edition*'. The F reading is given on the right of the square bracket.

I.1

    48 metal] mettle

I.2

   114 *marked as 'Scena Tertia' in* F
   172 sithe (*this edition*)] sigh

I.3

    10 cost a witless] cost, witlesse
 26–7 rod | Becomes more] rod | More
   43 it] in

I.4

    5 sisterhood] Sisterstood

II.1

   12 your] our
   39 brakes of vice] brakes of Ice

II.2

25, 161 God save] 'Saue
   99 where] here

II.4

    4 God] heauen
    9 seared] feared
   24 swoons] swounds
   45 God's (*this edition*)] heauens
   48 metal] mettle
   53 or] and
   94 all-binding law] all-building-Law
153–4 world | Aloud what man (*this edition*)] world aloud | What man

III.1

   55 me to hear them] them to heare me
   72 Though] Through

          94 enew] emmew.
          99 damnèd'st] damnest
         133 penury] periury

III.2
          23 eat, array] eate away
          37 Free from our] From our
          38 waist] wast
      44–5 extracting it clutched] extracting clutch'd
         143 dearer] deare
     171–2 He's not past it yet] He's now past it, yet
         209 See] Sea
         214 and it is] and as it is
         215 as it is] and as it is
         263 strings] stings

IV.1
           6 though] but
          53 and so have] and haue

IV.2
          55 yare] y'are
          98 lordship's] Lords
         140 reckless] wreaklesse

IV.3
          15 Forthright] *Forthlight*
          16 Shoe-tie] *Shootie*
          98 well-balanced] Weale-ballanc'd

IV.4
          24 so (*Dyce*)] of a

IV.5
           8 Valentius] *Valencius*

V.1
          13 our] your
          95 vile] vild
         168 her face] your face
         420 confiscation] confutation

2

The following stage directions (or parts of directions) do not
appear in F. Minor additions such as '*aside*', '*to Juliet*', '*sings*' are
not listed here.

II.1

    36 *Exit Provost*
  132 *Exit Angelo*
  201 *Exit Froth*
  262 *Exit Elbow*

II.2

    0 *and a*
    2 *Exit Servant*
   17 *Enter Servant*
   22 *Exit Servant*
  161 *Exeunt Isabella, Lucio, and Provost*

II.3

    0 *disguised as a friar*

II.4

   19 *Exit Servant*

III.1

    0 *as a friar*
   56 *Duke and Provost retire*
  154 *Going*
       Duke comes forward
  175 *Exit Claudio*
       Enter Provost

III.2

    0 *Pompey, and*
   81 *Exeunt Elbow, Pompey, and Officers*
  179 *Officers with Mistress Overdone*
  197 *Exeunt Officers with Mistress Overdone*
  248 *Exeunt Escalus and Provost*

IV.1

    6 *as a friar*
    9 *Exit Boy*
   58 *Mariana and Isabella*

IV.2

    0 *Pompey*
   57 *Pompey and Abhorson*
   66 *Knocking*
   67 *Exit Claudio*
   69 *as a friar*
   82 *Knocking*

  Exit Provost
 84 *Knocking*
 86 *Enter Provost*
104 *Exit Messenger*
117 PROVOST *reads*
203 *Exit with Provost*

IV.3

  0 *Pompey*
 23 *within*
 27 *within*
 45 *as a friar*
 63 *Exeunt Abhorson and Pompey*
 90 *Provost*
156 *Exit Isabella*

IV.4

 17 *Escalus*

IV.5

  0 *in his own habit*
 10 *Exit*

IV.6

  9 *Friar*

V.1

  0 *Provost, Officers, and*
 18 *Friar*
162 *Isabella is led off, guarded*
204 *She unveils*
251 *Exit Provost*
258 *Duke*
269 *Exit an Attendant*
276 *as a friar*
  and Officers
345 *The Provost lays hands on the Duke*
352 *He pulls off the Friar's hood, and discovers the Duke*
376 *Angelo, with Mariana, Friar Peter, and Provost*
396 *Friar*
440 *kneeling*
466 *Exit Provost*
474 *muffled, and*
486 *He unmuffles Claudio*

521 *Exeunt Officers with Lucio*
536 *Exeunt*

3

The following list of characters appears at the end of the text in the Folio.

The names of all the Actors.

Vincentio: the Duke.
Angelo, the Deputie.
Escalus, an ancient Lord.
Claudio, a yong Gentleman.
Lucio, a fantastique.
2. Other like Gentlemen.
Prouost.
Thomas.
Peter. } *2. Friers.*
Elbow, a simple Constable.

Froth, a foolish Gentleman.
Clowne.
Abhorson, an Executioner.
Barnardine, a dissolute prisoner.
Isabella, sister to Claudio.
Mariana, betrothed to Angelo.
Iuliet, beloued of Claudio.
Francisca, a Nun.
Mistris Ouer-don, a Bawd.

Commentary

Biblical references are to the Bishops' Bible (1568). The abbreviation 'F' is used for the first Folio (1623).

I.I

    0 *Duke*: The Duke's name is given as Vincentio in the 'names of all the Actors' appended to the F text (see p. 111).

    6 *lists*: Bounds.

  8–9 *But that, to your sufficiency, as your worth is able, | And let them work*: Possibly a line has been omitted. The general sense is: apply yourselves to your duties with a competence matching your authority.

   10 *terms*: Sessions.

   11 *pregnant*: Well-informed, resourceful.

   14 *warp*: Deviate.

   17 *with special soul*: With absolute conviction.

   20 *organs*: Instruments.

   29 *belongings*: Capabilities.

   30 *proper*: Exclusively.

 32–3 *Heaven doth with us . . . Not light them for themselves*: While this image has its roots in several New Testament verses (e.g. Matthew 5:14–16, Luke 8:16 or 11:33), it may also consciously echo King James's *Basilikon Doron* (1599), which pointed out that rulers were duty-bound to display their virtue: 'so to glister and shine before their people . . . that their persons as bright lamps of godliness and virtue may . . . give light to all their steps.'

36–40 *Nature never . . . thanks and use*: Nature never lends her
gifts without herself determining the use to which they
shall be put.

41 *advertise*: Instruct.

46 *first in question*: First under consideration.

48 *metal*: There is a quibble on 'metal' and 'mettle' (which
is the F reading) but the amended spelling better fits
the imagery of the passage.

51 *leavened*: Well-fermented, carefully considered.

54 *prefers itself*: Takes priority, goes on ahead.

61 *something on*: Part of.
the way: Your way.

67–72 *I love the people . . . affect it*: King James I notoriously
disliked crowds (as was shown by an incident in March
1604 when he had to take refuge in the Royal Exchange),
and there are comparable allusions at I.3.8–10 and
II.4.24–30. Taken with a possible echo of his *Basilikon
Doron* (see I.1.32–3), it may be that we are intended
from this opening scene to see the Duke as a version
of King James. He was patron of Shakespeare's acting
troupe, the King's Men, and *Measure for Measure* was
performed before him in December 1604, but how
important we think these facts are will depend on when
we think the play was written, and how we judge the
Duke within the play.

70 *aves*: Acclamations.

78 *the bottom of my place*: The basis of my duties.

83 *wait upon*: Attend.

I.2

o *Lucio*: In the list of characters added to the F text Lucio
is described as *a fantastique*. The word may imply a
fop, but in Lucio's case it seems more likely to signify
someone with an unbridled fantasy or imagination.

2 *composition*: Agreement.

15–16 *the petition . . . that prays for peace*: The regular form
of grace ended with the petition that God might 'send
us peace in Christ'.

27–8 *there went but a pair of shears between us*: We were cut
from the same cloth.

29 *lists*: Selvages (narrow strips discarded as waste when material is made up).

32 *three-piled*: Triple napped (the most expensive kind of velvet).

33 *kersey*: Coarse-woven woollen cloth.

 piled: The word puns on baldness and haemorrhoids, both regarded as a legacy of syphilis.

34 *French velvet*: This allusion to the best quality of velvet characteristically glances at 'the French disease' (syphilis) and 'velvet women' (prostitutes).

38–9 *forget to drink after thee*: Lucio will not expose himself to infection by drinking from the same cup.

43 *tainted or free*: With or without venereal infection.

49 *dolours*: There is a pun on 'dollars'.

51 *French crown*: The pun on baldness and 'the French disease' at 34 is repeated.

82 *the sweat*: Either the sweating sickness (a sixteenth-century epidemic) or else the sweating treatment given to victims of syphilis (see note to III.2.54).

83 *Enter Pompey*: In the conversation that follows, Mistress Overdone questions Pompey about *Yonder man* (usually assumed to be Claudio), although earlier, at 59–69, she had identified him, and knew that he had been arrested and why. Various explanations have been offered for this – that *Yonder man* is not Claudio, but someone else, also being arrested for fornication; that Mistress Overdone has not realized that Pompey is referring to Claudio; or that this passage of dialogue (81–114) was intended to replace her earlier dialogue with the two Gentlemen (59–80): John Jowett and Gary Taylor (*Shakespeare Reshaped*) have argued that it was a later addition, probably by Thomas Middleton, intended to supersede the dialogue between Mistress Overdone and Pompey (who are always *Bawd* and *Clown* in F).

92 *maid*: Young of fish (punning on *trouts* in line 89).

113 *provost*: An officer charged with apprehending and punishing offenders.

120–21 *Make us . . . it will*: The phrase *The words of heaven* seems to refer to Romans 9:15: 'For [God] saith to Moses

"I will have mercy on whom I will have mercy'" (words
often used to justify the Calvinist doctrine of election
or pre-destination); but *pay down . . . by weight* also
recalls the Mosaic law of 'an eye for an eye', the doctrine
of strict punishment, rejected by Christ in the Sermon
on the Mount (and a central issue in *Measure for
Measure*).

126 *scope*: Liberty.

128 *ravin*: Devour voraciously.

   proper bane: Particular poison.

132 *lief*: Willingly.

   foppery: Foolishness.

133 *mortality*: Sometimes emended to 'morality', but this
word does not appear in Shakespeare, and *mortality* is
suitable enough for early modern prisons, with their
high death rates.

143 *looked after*: Kept close watch upon.

146 *She is fast my wife*: Juliet was Claudio's wife by virtue
of hand-fasting or pre-contract, though the marriage
had not yet been solemnized.

147 *denunciation*: Public announcement.

149 *propagation*: Augmentation.

152 *made them for us*: Brought them to our point of view.

164 *I stagger in*: I am uncertain.

171 *tickle*: Precariously.

172 *sithe*: Sigh, also meaning to separate milk curds from
whey (as in cheese-making) and punning on 'scythe'.

177 *approbation*: Probation.

182 *prone*: Quick, eager.

   dialect: Language. Claudio's hope that Isabella's body-
language may 'move' the Justice is fulfilled – and with
almost disastrous consequences.

189 *tick-tack*: A game in which pegs were driven into holes;
here used to signify sexual intercourse.

I.3

3 *complete*: So constituted as to be impenetrable.

10 *Where youth and cost a witless bravery keeps*: Where
youth and wealth put on a mindless display. The F
reading *Where youth and cost, witless bravery keeps* would

mean 'where youth and wealth (and) mindless display are (to be found)'.

12 *stricture*: Strictness.

20 *weeds*: Some editors amend to 'steeds' (though the laws can scarcely apply to horses), and others to 'wills'. Shakespeare, however, was not averse to mixed metaphors, and links *weeds* with bits or curbs on at least four other occasions.

21 *fourteen*: This is not consistent with Claudio's *nineteen ʒodiacs* at I.2.167 and may have arisen from misreading of a numeral, either arabic or roman.

28 *Dead to infliction*: No longer able to be invoked.

29–31 *And liberty . . . decorum*: The violation of order or degree is a recurring theme with Shakespeare, whose ironic exposition of the doctrine is presented in *Troilus and Cressida*, I.3.75–137.

35 *Sith*: Since.

41–3 *Who may . . . slander*: Who may, lurking behind my title, take effective action, while avoiding bringing slander on my authority in the process.

50 *precise*: Rigidly puritanical.

51 *at a guard with envy*: On his guard against malice.

53 *Is more to bread than stone*: An echo of Matthew 7:9: 'Or what man is there of you, whom if his son ask bread, will he give him a stone.'

54 *seemers*: Shakespeare often uses 'seem' in the sense of 'pretend' or 'dissemble', and the present usage strongly suggests that Vincentio already suspects Angelo of hypocrisy – an interpretation which receives powerful support from the revelations in III.1.

I.4

5 *the votarists of Saint Clare*: The order of the Poor Clares, founded in 1212 by St Francis of Assisi and St Clare, imposed a life of poverty, service and contemplation. It had not, of course, functioned in England after the Dissolution of the Monasteries in 1536–9, but Shakespeare shows a close knowledge of its regulations.

17 *stead*: Assist.

25 *weary*: Tedious.

30 *make me not your story*: Do not tell me false tales.

32 *lapwing*: The lapwing runs to and fro in order to conceal the location of its nest. Shakespeare, here and in *Much Ado About Nothing*, III.1.24–5, seems to associate the bird with tittle-tattle and amorous intrigue.

39 *Fewness and truth*: To be brief and truthful.

42 *seedness*: State of being sown.

43 *foison*: Harvest.

51–2 *Bore many gentlemen . . . action*: Rumours of war are current in the early part of the play (see I.2.1–5, 81) but Shakespeare fails to develop them. Their purpose is presumably to establish that Lucio and his friends are aimless semi-military characters not unlike those in *All's Well that Ends Well*.

54 *giving-out were*: Announcement was (*were* is probably subjunctive singular, within indirect speech).

60 *rebate*: Make dull.

70 *my pith of business*: The main purpose of my business.

72 *censured*: Condemned.

75–6 *Alas . . . good*: Most editors print an interrogation mark after *good*, but the F pointing, which conveys Isabella's conviction of her own helplessness, seems convincing.

82–3 *All their petitions are as freely theirs | As they themselves would owe them*: All their *petitions* are granted as *freely* as if they themselves had the granting of them.

86 *Mother*: Prioress.

II.1

6 *fall*: Let fall.

12 *your*: F reads *our*, which, on the assumption that *our blood* relates to human nature in general, may be correct.

19 *passing on*: Passing sentence on.

22–3 *what knows . . . thieves*: What does the law itself know of the judgements that have been passed on thieves by other thieves? Line 22 is, however, metrically suspicious, and it may be that the requisite reading is 'what man knows' or 'what judge knows'.

23 *pregnant*: Obvious, convincing.

28 *For*: Because.

36 *pilgrimage*: Span of life.

39 *brakes of vice*: F's *brakes of Ice* is one of the most notorious cruxes in the play and has never been satisfactorily explained. Editors have usually taken 38–40 as
thoughts (line 38 is printed in italics in F), have glossed
brakes as 'thickets' and have explained *and answer none*
as 'refuse to be accountable'. 'Ice' is often emended to
'vice' (assuming a phonetic error), in which case, the
meaning might be that some people often misbehave
and get away with it, while others are punished the first
time they break the rules. An alternative reading,
emending 'brakes' to 'breaks' of ice, would mean that
some people survive even though they break the ice
many times, while others are caught the first time they
do so. To 'break the ice' could also mean to have sex
with a virgin.

56 *comes off well*: Is well-spoken.

61 *parcel-bawd*: Part-time bawd.

64 *hot-house*: Bath-house (and, by implication, a brothel).

66 *detest*: That is, protest.

77 *cardinally*: That is, carnally.

85 *misplaces*: Misuses words.

87 *stewed prunes*: Linked with brothels (known as 'stews'),
and used either to prevent or cure syphilis; a dish set
in the window was a sign of a brothel, but it could also
signify the prostitutes themselves – hence Pompey's
apology.

113 *Come me to*: Come to.

120 *Allhallond Eve*: All-hallow's Eve (31 October).

122 *a lower chair*: The precise significance of *a lower chair*
has never been satisfactorily defined, and editors usually
make sceptical reference to George Steevens's assertion that most houses formerly had a 'low chair' for
the use of the sick or the lazy.

123 *Bunch of Grapes*: The name of a room in an inn.

125 *an open room*: A public room.

140 *this gentleman's face*: Froth's countenance is evidently
the subject of the jokes which extend to 151. It is
conceivable that, like Bardolph in the historical plays,

he was given a very red face – 'Lucifer's privy-kitchen, where he doth nothing but roast malt-worms' (*Henry IV, Part II*, II.4.328–9).

148 *supposed*: That is, deposed.

154 *an it like you*: If it please you.
    respected: That is, suspected.

164 *Justice or Iniquity*: Escalus refers to Elbow, who like other constables in Elizabethan drama, is notably stupid, and to Pompey, who is likened to Iniquity, sometimes the name of the Vice in Tudor morality plays. The scene also includes an actual Justice, though he remains silent until 264.

167 *Hannibal*: Elbow produces his own characteristic misnomer for 'cannibal', but the subsequent jokes linking Pompey with Julius Caesar show that a deliberate allusion to the Carthaginian general is intended here.

195–6 *and you will hang them*: Escalus, playing on the phrase 'hang, draw and quarter' (a horrible form of public execution) assures Froth that, if he cultivates the acquaintance of tapsters, they will draw his money from him, and he will cry, 'Hang them!'

199 *taphouse*: Tavern.

207 *your bum*: Thickly stuffed trunk-hose were fashionable at the time when *Measure for Measure* was written.

208–9 *Pompey the Great*: Cnaius Pompeius Magnus (106–48 BC). He was defeated by Julius Caesar in the battle of Pharsalia, and this is alluded to later in the scene (236–8).

210 *colour it*: Camouflage it.

219 *splay*: Sterilize.

223 *take order*: Take action.

226 *heading*: Beheading.

231 *bay*: The part of a house that lies under a single gable.

237 *shrewd*: Harsh.

264 *Eleven, sir*: The Justice, who remains oddly silent until this moment, informs us that it is the eleventh hour (with obvious symbolism), and that *Lord Angelo is severe* (269). His silence may suggest that true justice has been

suppressed in Vienna (cf. the Justices Shallow and
Silence in *Henry IV, Part II*).

II.2

25 *God save*: The F line as it stands is metrically defective
and the reading *'Saue* is suspicious. If, as is likely,
Shakespeare wrote 'God save', the scribe, Ralph Crane,
would have omitted 'God' in accordance with the Act
of Abuses of 1606 (which forbade the naming of God
on the stage).

35–6 *I do beseech you, let it be his fault, | And not my brother*:
I beseech you let my brother's fault, not my brother,
be condemned to death.

40 *To fine . . . record*: To punish the *faults* whose *fine*
(penalty) has already been established by law.

52 *Look what*: Most editors print 'Look, what', which indicates an impatient exclamation, but there is no comma
in F and it is possible that Shakespeare intended the
idiomatic use of *look what*, meaning 'whatever'.

59 *longs*: Belongs.

65 *slipped*: Erred.

76 *the top of judgement*: God, the ultimate judge.

79 *Like man new made*: Like man at the Creation, before
sin had crept into the world. Mercy is seen as part of
the breath of life which God breathed into the nostrils
of Adam (Genesis 2:7).

90 *The law hath not been dead, though it hath slept*: The
legal maxim '*Dormiunt aliquando leges, moriuntur
nunquam*' is attributed to Sir Edward Coke.

95 *a glass*: Either a crystal, as commonly used by fortune-
tellers, or 'a glass prospective' of the kind used with
spectacular effect in Robert Greene's *Friar Bacon and
Friar Bungay* (1594).

96 *by remissness, new-conceived*: As the result of (further)
leniency, just conceived.

112 *pelting*: Insignificant.

120 *glassy*: As frail as glass – or perhaps as invisible as glass,
or as reflective.

123 *laugh mortal*: Laugh so much that they became
human beings ('mortals') – if they had spleens like us.

126 *We cannot weigh our brother with ourself*: We cannot use the same standard to judge ourselves and other people.

132 *Art advised o'that*: Have you discovered that? Lucio is himself a soldier of sorts, and, though Isabella's assurance that *Great men may jest with saints* (127) touches him not, he is perhaps surprised by her knowledge of army procedure.

136 *skins the vice o'th'top*: Covers the vice on the top with a new skin.

149 *sicles*: Shekels.

153 *preservèd souls*: The souls of those preserved from evil, that is, Isabella's sister nuns.

159 *Where prayers cross*: Where prayers are at cross-purposes.

165–8 *but it is I . . . virtuous season*: The warm sunshine of the *virtuous season*, or flowering time, causes the *violet* (Isabella) to flourish, but corrupts the *carrion* (Angelo) lying beside it.

169 *sense*: Sensual desire.

172 *evils*: Privies (with a sense of desecrating sacred ground).

187 *fond*: Infatuated.

II.3

11 *flaws*: Unruly passions.

12 *blistered her report*: Sullied her reputation.

23 *hollowly*: Falsely.

30–34 *but least you do repent . . . stand in fear*: The syntax here is difficult: adopting the F reading *least* (rather than 'lest'), and assuming that *you do* means 'you ought to', the Duke advises Juliet, 'You should repent the least that your sin has brought you to this shame, for that kind of sorrow is always for ourselves, and not for heaven, showing that we refrain from offending God not so much out of love for Him as out of fear of Him.' Reading 'lest' for 'least' gives an unfinished statement, interrupted by Juliet. It begins 'But unless you repent that your sin has brought you to this shame with genuine regret, for such regret is always for ourselves, and not for heaven, showing that we refrain from offending

God not so much out of love for Him as out of fear of Him...' These two readings imply different versions of the character of the Friar/Duke.

II.4

3 *invention*: Thought.

4 *God*: The word 'God' never appears in the F text, though 'heaven' appears frequently, and it is usually assumed that the word 'heaven' has replaced 'God' throughout the play, as a result of the Act of Abuses of 1606. In this example, *God* must have been the original word, since the following line refers to *His name* (see also II.4.45).

9 *gravity*: Staidness.

12 *for vain*: In vain (with a possible pun on 'vane').
   place: Position of authority.

13 *case*: Outer covering.

16–17 *Let's write ... the devil's crest*: The general sense is that, even if we write *good Angel* on the *devil's horn*, it won't change his (devilish) nature, and as a motto, *good Angel* is not part of the *devil's crest*, that is, his distinctive heraldic device.

27 *The general*: The populace.
   a well-wished king: This is a more obvious compliment to James I than the references at I.1.67–72 and I.3.7–10.

45 *saucy*: Lecherous.
   coin God's image: Beget bastard children.
   God's image: F reads *heauens Image*, which blurs a palpable allusion to Genesis 1:27. Here, as at 4, it is a ready inference that the Act of Abuses led to a modification.

48 *in restrainèd means*: By forbidden methods.

57–8 *Our compelled sins | Stand more for number than for accompt*: The *sins* which we cannot help committing are reckoned by *number* rather than by weight.
   accompt: Account.

73 *And nothing of your answer*: And nothing for which you are answerable.

75 *crafty*: This might be either an adjective or an adverb, while *so* may go with *seem* or intensify *crafty*. Emending

to 'craftily' improves the metre but limits the meanings.

76 *Let be ignorant . . . good*: Leave out *ignorant* and (assume
I am) in nothing good. Emending to 'Let me be ignorant' makes Isabella prefer the first of Angelo's alternatives, but her assertion that she is *in nothing good* suggests that she accepts the second.

79 *these black masks*: Editors have assumed that Angelo alludes to the masks worn by women members of the audience, but direct reference of this kind is rare in Shakespeare. The dramatic effect is enhanced if we take the *black masks* to signify Isabella's veil (the Poor Clares wear a black veil), and this gives point to *enshield* at 80.

80 *enshield*: Shielded, defended (see preceding note).

90 *But in the loss of question*: Except for the sake of argument.

94 *all-binding law*: F's *all-building-Law* makes reasonable sense, but *manacles* in 93 justifies the emendation.

111 *Ignomy*: Ignominy.

112 *two houses*: Different stock.

122 *fedary*: Confederate.

123 *Owe and succeed thy weakness*: Own and inherit that frailty which you attribute to all men.

127–8 *Men their creation mar | In profiting by them*: Men who profit by women's frailty debase their own place in creation. Woman was thought of as being part of man (Genesis 2:21–3).

134 *arrest*: Take you at.

147 *To pluck on others*: To test other people.

160 *now I give my sensual race the rein*: I now give free rein to my sensual inclinations. There is probably a pun on horse-riding which, in Elizabethan usage, is often given a sexual connotation.

162 *prolixious*: Superfluous.

178 *prompture*: Prompting.

III.1

5–41 *Be absolute . . . all even*: In this speech the Duke bids Claudio reflect on the comforts of death in case it should

be his lot to die – but, in accordance with the character
that he assumes for the greater part of the play, he does
not disclose that it is his purpose that Claudio shall live.
It is surprising, given the Duke's disguise, that the
consolation he offers is classical and Stoic, rather than
Christian.

5 *absolute*: Resolved.

10 *keep'st*: Dwellest.

14 *accommodations*: Equipment, endowments.

17 *worm*: Snake.

24–5 *For thy complexion shifts to strange effects,* | *After the
moon*: The influence of the moon affects your behaviour (thus rendering you *not certain*, that is, mutable,
and subject to capricious desires).

26 *ingots*: Bars of gold or silver.

29 *bowels*: Offspring.

31 *serpigo*: Psoriasis, any spreading skin disease.

34–6 *for all thy . . . palsied eld*: These obscure lines have been
variously explained. The general sense seems to be that
blessed youth turns to unblessed old age, to the state
of helplessness (Sans teeth, sans eyes, sans taste, sans
everything) which renders man wholly dependent on
the charity of others. But the passage may be corrupt,
and it is a ready inference that F's *aged* is a misprint
for 'agued'.

37 *limb*: Strength of limb.

62 *leiger*: Resident ambassador.

63 *appointment*: Preparations.

72 *vastidity*: Vastness.

73 *determined scope*: Confined limit.

78 *entertain*: Of the various possible meanings, 'cherish'
(*Oxford English Dictionary* entertain, v.11) seems the
most apt.

92 *appliances*: Expedients.

94 *enew*: Drive into the water. The verb relates to the way
in which hawks kill their prey. F reads *emmew*, which
some editors take to signify 'inmew', that is, coop up.

96 *cast*: Vomited.

97, 100 *princely*: F reads *prenzie*, a word that occurs only in

these two lines. It has been derived from an obsolete
Italian word for prince ('*prenze*'), and the sense *princely*
seems most probable (forms such as '*prence*' occur
in sixteenth-century Scots), although it might be
connected with '*primsie*' (over-fastidious), another
Scots word that appears 200 years later. To add to the
difficulties, F's punctuation suggests that *prenzie* is used
as a noun at 97 and an adjective at 100, where it describes
guards (that is, trimmings on clothes). Some editors
emend to '*precise*', but this seems less likely as a descrip-
tion of '*guards*'.

111 *affections*: Passions.

113 *force*: Enforce.

118 *perdurably fined*: Punished eternally.

122 *cold obstruction*: Rigor mortis.

124 *delighted*: Capable of feeling delight.

125–31 *To bathe . . . horrible*: Claudio's 'dream of death' closely
resembles that of Hamlet (III.1.56–88), and its simi-
larities to Dante's *Inferno* and Milton's Hell have
often been remarked upon. But Claudio's meditations
are upon Purgatory rather than Hell since he is, by
inference, a Catholic, like his sister. The play makes it
clear that he is to receive shrift, and there is no reason
to suppose that he anticipates total damnation, though
his thoughts may turn that way in 129–31, which, as
they stand in F, are not susceptible of satisfactory
explanation.

126 *thrilling*: Piercing.

144 *shield*: Grant that, ensure that.

145 *wilderness*: Wildness.

146 *defiance*: Rejection, declaration of aversion.

164–6 *only he hath made an assay of her virtue . . . disposition
of natures*: He has made a trial of her virtue only in
order to test his ability to judge character.

180 *habit*: Robes.

185 *complexion*: Nature.

191 *resolve*: Inform.

195 *discover*: Expose.

198 *avoid*: Repudiate.

210 *fearful*: Afraid.

217 *limit of the solemnity*: Date fixed for the solemnization.

224 *combinate*: Betrothed.

228 *pretending*: Falsely alleging.

235 *avail*: Benefit.

246 *refer yourself to this advantage*: Impose this condition.

251 *stead up*: Serve to keep (or, go instead of).

252 *encounter*: Sexual assignation.

255 *scaled*: Weighed, as on scales, or else, stripped of (fish-) scales or outer layers (and so to appear as he really is).

256 *frame*: Prime.

262 *holding up*: Maintaining.

264 *presently*: Immediately.

III.2

Most editors break the Act at this point, thus imposing a distinction which did not exist on the Shakespearian stage. Since there is no reason for supposing that the Duke leaves the stage, even momentarily, adherence to F seems amply justified, but for convenience of reference the conventional scene division is indicated in the margin.

3 *bastard*: A sweet Spanish wine (with, of course, an obvious pun).

5 *two usuries*: The *worser* usury is money-lending; the *merriest* is fleshmongering.

8 *fox and lamb skins*: Gowns trimmed with fox fur and lined with lamb skin were apparently worn by money-lenders in Shakespeare's day.

9 *stands for the facing*: Acts as (represents, supports) the facing, that is, the turned back, visible portion of the garment (also appearance, or deceit). The lamb skin is worn on the inside, the fox fur decorates the outside, and indicates the usurer's craftiness.

37 *seeming*: Dissembling.

38 *a cord*: Elbow puns on two meanings, (1) the hangman's rope, (2) the girdle which is part of the Duke's Franciscan habit.

43 *Pygmalion's images*: Pygmalion, according to classical

mythology, brought his sculpture of a woman to life
when he fell in love with it: *newly made woman* could
mean a recently made sculpture, or a sculpture recently
transformed into a woman, as well as a girl who has
just reached puberty, or has recently lost her virginity.

44–5 *extracting it clutched*: Holding money in it.

46 *tune*: Fashion.

47 *trot*: The word usually signifies an old woman, which,
in one sense, is what Pompey is. The possibility of a
misprint for 'troth' cannot be ruled out.

48 *Is it sad, and few words*: Lucio asks whether melancholy
is now the fashion. The play was written at about the
time when the character of the 'malcontent' was in
vogue.

49 *trick*: Fashion.

51–2 *Procures*: Pimps.

54 *tub*: There is a pun on (1) the salting of beef, (2) the
sweating treatment for the cure of venereal disease.

56 *powdered*: Pickled.

57 *unshunned*: Inevitable.

67 *husband*: Housekeeper.

70 *wear*: Fashion.

72 *mettle*: There is a pun on 'metal' – the iron of the
shackles that Pompey will wear in prison.

102 *sea-maid*: Mermaid.

103 *stock-fishes*: Dried cod. Monstrous births of the kind
glanced at by Lucio were a favourite theme in ballads
and pamphlets of the period.

105 *motion generative*: A puppet (*motion*) with organs of
generation. Lewis Theobald suggested emending to
'ungenerative', which would anticipate Lucio's *ungenitured* at 163–4. In Act V, scene 5 of Ben Jonson's
Bartholomew Fair (1614), the puritan minister and the
'motion' (i.e. the puppet) dispute, and the puppet
confutes the minister's attack on theatrical cross-
dressing by pointing out that 'we have neither male nor
female amongst us' (in other words, that a 'motion'
cannot be 'generative').

106 *infallible*: Unquestionable.

109 *cod-piece*: The name given to the flap worn in the front of hose for covering the genitals. The word sometimes refers, as apparently here, to the genitals themselves.

115 *detected for*: Charged with.

120 *use*: Custom.

   clack-dish: Beggars carried a wooden bowl for the reception of alms. This had a movable lid which they clacked in order to attract notice. Lucio perhaps uses the word in a bawdy, figurative sense.

121 *crotchets*: Peculiarities.

124 *inward*: Intimate.

130 *the greater file of the subject*: The majority of the people.

132 *unweighing*: Undiscriminating.

134 *helmed*: Directed.

135 *upon a warranted need*: If it were genuinely needed.

135–6 *proclamation*: Reputation.

136–7 *bringings-forth*: Achievements.

138–9 *unskilfully*: In ignorance.

156 *opposite*: Opponent.

162 *tun-dish*: A funnel – a metaphor for sexual intercourse.

163–4 *ungenitured*: Without testicles.

169 *untrussing*: Letting down his hose.

171 *would eat mutton*: Would not fast on Fridays; would have sex with prostitutes (*mutton* suggests age and toughness).

172 *mouth*: Kiss erotically.

175 *mortality*: Human life.

193 *Philip and Jacob*: The Feast of St Philip and St James (1 May).

213 *dissolution*: Total destruction.

214–16 *and it is . . . undertaking*: And it is as *dangerous* to continue in any *course* of action, *as it is virtuous to be constant* . . . Emending 'constant' to 'inconstant' gives the Duke's words an ironic turn.

217–18 *security enough to make fellowships accursed*: Social relationships are cursed by the frequency with which men stand surety for their friends. Vincentio's seemingly casual comment links with the central theme of such plays as *The Merchant of Venice* and *Timon of Athens*.

228 *events*: The outcome of his enterprises.

232 *sinister*: Unjust.

240 *shore*: Limit.

249–70 The Duke's soliloquy, written in rhyming couplets, changes the play's rhythm, and allows him to sum up what has happened so far, and to outline his plan for the rest of the action.

252 *and*: If.

253–4 *More nor less to others paying | Than by self-offences weighing*: Passing judgement on others in accordance with his own imperfections.

258 *my vice*: The vice that I have allowed to grow up.

261–4 *How may likeness . . . substantial things*: These lines, sometimes held to be corrupt, are certainly cryptic. F prints them as a question, but they seem more likely to be an apostrophe. The *likeness made in crimes* is the resemblance between the crimes of Claudio and Angelo, which have made *practice on the times*, that is, they have deceived people. *To-draw* may mean 'to draw apart' with the spiders' strings of the law *Most ponderous and substantial things* (for example, the relationship of man and wife, perhaps).

IV.1

1–6 *Take, O take . . . in vain*: This song also appears in *Rollo, Duke of Normandy*, also known as *The Bloody Brother* (1616–19) by John Fletcher and others, where it is followed by a second stanza. The composer John Wilson set these words to music, and the song appears in his manuscript song-book, but since Wilson was only born in 1595, it is highly probable that this song was added at a later performance of the play. John Jowett and Gary Taylor (in *Shakespeare Reshaped, 1606–23*) argue persuasively that an adapter introduced a stanza from this popular song from *Rollo* some years after Shakespeare's death. The version supplied by F includes some repeats and has *but* instead of *though* in the last line. The second stanza makes explicit that the song is sung by a man to a woman:

> Hide, O hide those hills of snow
>   That thy frozen bosom bears,
> On whose tops the pinks that grow
>   Are yet of those that April wears.
> But first set my poor heart free,
> Bound in those icy chains by thee.

Wilson's setting of both stanzas is reprinted and usefully discussed in Lever's Arden edition, pp. 201–3.

27 *circummured*: Walled round.

29 *planchèd*: Planked.

30 *his*: Its.

39 *In action all of precept*: This difficult phrase presumably means that Angelo directed Isabella by means of hints, gestures and perhaps sketch-maps.

41 *observance*: Compliance.

43 *possessed*: Informed.

59–64 *O place and greatness . . . in their fancies*: The Duke's seemingly gratuitous meditation is, as Johnson noted, 'a necessity to fill up the time in which the ladies conversed apart'. The sentiments are characteristically Shakespearian and the imagery accords with the concept of '*Rumour, painted full of tongues*' in the Induction to *Henry IV, Part II*.

60–61 *Volumes of report . . . quest*: Quantities of these reports follow a false scent (*Run . . . false*) and bark as if they had picked up the scent, even though they are heading in the wrong direction (*contrarious quest*).

64 *rack*: Put on the rack.

71 *He is your husband on a pre-contract*: The contract between Angelo and Mariana, according to the Duke, belonged to the category of *sponsalia jurata* and could not be dissolved without the consent of both parties.

74 *flourish*: Adorn.

75 *yet our tithe's to sow*: Our seed remains to be sown; 'tithe' was the tenth part of a harvest, due to the church, and here refers to the corn sown from tithe dues, or merely 'seed'.

IV.2

4 *his wife's head*: In Pauline doctrine the husband is the head of the wife (Ephesians 5:23). There is perhaps a pun on maidenheads, as in *Romeo and Juliet*, I.1.21–5.

6 *snatches*: Quibbles.

11 *gyves*: Fetters.

12–13 *unpitied*: Pitiless.

18 *Abhorson*: The name is a curious portmanteau one which combines the words 'abhor' and 'whoreson' and may also pun on 'abortion'.

21 *compound*: Make terms.

26 *mystery*: Profession.

30 *favour*: Face.

40 *Every true man's apparel fits your thief*: This argument is difficult to follow, though the general sense seems to be that the honest man thinks any clothes are more than good enough for the thief, while the thief thinks that none of them are good enough for him – *fit* means both to be the right size (as clothes should be), and to 'suit' or 'satisfy'. But it is odd that Abhorson replies to Pompey's demand for proof that hanging *is a mystery* ('a skilled trade or profession', and also a secret, as today) by talking about thieves who steal clothes, instead of about hangmen who were permitted to claim their victims' clothes. It is also odd that Pompey seems to provide so much of the *proof* himself, and many editors have reassigned his words to Abhorson.

41 *true*: Honest.

55 *yare*: Prepared.

55–6 *a good turn*: A hangman was said to turn off his victims when he removed the ladder from under their feet.

64 *starkly*: Stiffly.

77 *Even with*: In exact conformity with.
stroke and line: Straight line or course, but perhaps also suggesting the *stroke* of the executioner's axe, and the *line* of the hangman's rope.

80 *qualify*: Reduce.
mealed: Stained.

84 *steelèd*: Hardened.

86 *th'unsisting postern*: The unresisting or unassisting small back or side door – often emended to 'th'unshifting postern', meaning 'unyielding'.

89 *countermand*: Reprieve.

95 *siege*: Seat.

107 *quick celerity*: Sharp or lively speed.

114 *putting on*: Incitement.

133 *fact*: Offence.

142 *mortality*: Death.
desperately mortal: In a desperate state of mortal sin.

153 *cunning*: Discernment.

158 *present*: Immediate.

161 *limited*: Prescribed.

168–9 *discover the favour*: Recognize the features.

171 *tie the beard*: So that it looks shorter, though some editors emend to 'dye' or 'trim', or omit *tie* altogether.

183 *fearful*: Afraid.

184 *attempt*: Tempt.

187 *character*: Handwriting.

196 *th'unfolding star*: The morning star (the signal for the shepherd to lead his flock from the fold).

202 *resolve*: Reassure.

IV.3

2 *house of profession*: Brothel.

5 *commodity*: Usurers, in order to obtain more than the lawful interest of ten per cent, devised the system of lending commodities for resale. The various commodities mentioned by Elizabeth writers include lute-strings, hobby-horses, morris-bells and, as here, *ginger* and *brown paper*.

6 *five marks*: A mark was a coin worth 13*s*. 4*d*., two-thirds of a pound. Money-lenders could demand that borrowers purchased a *commodity*, a quantity of (often worthless) goods, in this instance *brown paper and old ginger*. Master Rash promised to pay £197 for them, and received £5 6*s*. 8*d*. in ready money, but he could not resell the brown paper and ginger (old women were supposed to like ginger).

11 *peaches*: Denounces, informs against (someone) for being (something).

13 *Copperspur*: Shakespeare evidently recalled, perhaps unconsciously, that a character named Copper appears in George Whetstone's *1 Promos and Cassandra*, V.5.

15 *tilter*: Jouster, fencer.

16 *Shoe-tie*: This was apparently a nickname given to travellers, many of whom wore on their shoes the elaborate rosettes fashionable abroad.

18 *for the Lord's sake*: This was the customary formula used by prisoners for begging alms from passers-by.

39 *clap into*: Make haste with.

46 *ghostly father*: Spiritual father, confessor.

53 *billets*: Thick sticks.

61 *ward*: Cell.

66 *transport him*: Send him to his doom.

71 *omit*: Ignore.

76 *presently*: Immediately.

77 *Prefixed*: Stipulated.

82 *continue*: Preserve.

87 *journal*: Daily.

yond generation: There have been various attempts to emend or explain this difficult phrase. Perhaps the best explanation is that it refers to the world that lies beyond the darkness of the prison (which never receives the sun's greeting).

89 *free*: Willing.

98–9 *By cold gradation . . . with Angelo*: Step by step (or in due order of seniority), observing the proper procedures.

proceed: Either 'walk' or 'take legal action (against)'.

103 *want*: Require.

117 *close*: Silent.

127 *covent*: Convent.

128 *instance*: Indication.

131 *pace*: Direct, train (as a horse).

133 *bosom*: Wishes.

140 *perfect him*: Relate to him in full.

141 *to the head*: To the face.

143 *combinèd*: Bound.

151 *fain*: Glad, or forced.

152–3 *for my head*: For fear of being beheaded.

153 *set me to't*: Arouse my sexual desires.

155 *fantastical*: Whimsical.

157 *beholding*: Indebted.

160 *woodman*: Woman-chaser.

170 *medlar*: Prostitute.

IV.4

1 *disvouched*: Contradicted.

5 *reliver*: Hand over. Most editors, following Edward Capell, print 're-deliver', but F's *re-liuer* (from French *relivrer*) is a typical Shakespearian coinage.

11 *devices*: False charges.

15 *men of sort and suit*: Men of rank and others normally attendant on the Duke.

18 *unpregnant*: Unready.

24 *bears so credent bulk*: Carries such a weight of conviction.

credent: Credible.

27 *sense*: Sharp perception or feeling (perhaps glancing at Claudio's sensuality).

IV.5

1 *deliver me*: Deliver for me.

3 *keep*: Follow.

4 *drift*: Plan.

5 *blench*: Deviate.

8 *Crassus*: Shakespeare evidently picked up the name from Whetstone's *Heptameron* which alludes to 'the two brave Romanes, Marcus Crassus, and Marius'. This also warrants the surmise that *Varrius* may have been a scribal or compositorial error for 'Marius', though such an assumption is far from necessary. The names introduced in this scene well illustrate that Shakespearian 'confusion of the names and manners of different times' which Johnson (wrongly) condemned in *Cymbeline*.

IV.6

4 *to veil full purpose*: To conceal the full plan.

10 *stand*: Position.

13 *generous*: Of noble birth.

14 *hent*: Taken their places at.

V.I

0 *at several doors*: The Jacobean stage had doors at either side, and to these there attached a rough but effective symbolism. The Duke, Varrius and attendant Lords would enter by the one door, the remaining characters by the other.

1 *cousin*: A form of address used by a sovereign to noblemen.

8 *Forerunning more requital*: Preceding other rewards.
bonds: Obligations.

10 *To lock it in the wards of covert bosom*: To imprison it in my innermost heart.

13 *razure*: Erasure.
Give we our hand: F has *Give we your hand*, often emended to 'Give me your hand', but the royal plural seems more in keeping with the formality of the occasion.

16 *keep*: Dwell.

20 *Vail your regard*: Lower your eyes.

48 *conjure*: Adjure.

50–51 *That thou neglect me not with that opinion | That I am touched with madness*: That you do not ignore me because you suppose that I am demented.

52 *unlike*: Unlikely.

54 *absolute*: Perfect.

56 *dressings*: Robes of office.
characts: Insignia.

65 *inequality*: Injustice.

67 *seems*: That seems.

70 *upon*: On account of.

82 *perfect*: Fully prepared.

90 *to the matter*: Pertinent.

94 *refelled*: Refuted.

98 *concup'scible*: Sensual.
intemperate: Ungoverned.

100 *remorse*: Compassion.

105 *fond*: Foolish.

107 *practice*: Conspiracy.

108 *it imports no reason*: It does not make sense.

110 *proper*: Applicable.

118 *countenance*: The word is variously explained as 'priv-
    ilege', 'pretence', but the requisite meaning may be
    'acceptance' (cf. the common Elizabethan verb 'to
    countenance').

126 *A ghostly father, belike*: Since the title *Friar Lodowick*
    signifies that he is a ghostly, or spiritual, father, the
    Duke must intend an ironical pun. Hence *ghostly* here
    means 'non-existent'.

130 *swinged*: Thrashed, beaten.

131 *This'*: This is.

145 *a temporary meddler*: A meddler in temporal (as opposed
    to spiritual) affairs.

157 *probation*: Proof.

158 *convented*: Summoned.

160 *vulgarly*: Publicly.

179 *punk*: Prostitute.

186 *known*: Had sexual knowledge of.

209 *match*: Appointment.

217 *proportions*: Dowry.

218 *composition*: The agreed sum.

219–20 *disvalued | In levity*: Discredited for wantonness.

231 *I did but smile till now*: Angelo's smile has already been
    mentioned at II.2.186–7. Both passages have sinister
    reverberations and suggest that the image of 'the smiler
    with a knife' was, for Shakespeare, a deeply personal
    one. Examples occur elsewhere in the plays, notably in
    Hamlet, I.5.108: 'That one may smile, and smile, and
    be a villain.'

234 *informal*: Demented.

240 *Compact*: Confederate.

243 *approbation*: Proof.

254 *your injuries*: The matters alleged against you.

257 *Determined*: Reached a judgement.

261 *Cucullus non facit monachum*: The hood does not make
    the monk. This proverb, signifying that appearances

can be deceptive, also occurs in *Twelfth Night*, I.5.50–51.

265 *enforce*: Urge.

266 *notable fellow*: Both words were often used in a pejorative sense, and here signify a 'notorious rascal'.

274 *handled her privately*: Lucio's tasteless sexual puns contrast oddly with his view of Isabella as *a thing enskied and sainted* at I.4.34, but he is, of course, the complete opportunist.

277 *darkly*: Cunningly.

278 *light*: Wanton.

290–91 *Respect to your great place, and let the devil | Be sometime honoured for his burning throne*: These lines have been much disputed and the F text may be corrupt. But 'and' in Shakespearian English sometimes stands for 'and also' or 'and even', and either of these senses would be appropriate here. The Duke is openly defiant, and what he is, in effect, saying is: I am willing to honour your authority and even that of the devil himself.

291 *burning throne*: The lines in *Antony and Cleopatra*, II.2.196–7, 'The barge she sat in, like a burnished throne, | Burned on the water', suggest that Shakespeare was as much concerned with the actual splendour of the devil's seat as with the more usual implications of hell-fire.

299 *retort*: Throw back.

306 *proper*: Very.

307 *glance*: Turn.

309 *touse*: Tear.

311 *hot*: Hasty.

314 *provincial*: Subject to local jurisdiction.

317 *stew*: The word, part of Vincentio's hell-broth imagery, also puns on 'stew' meaning brothel.

319–20 *Stand like the forfeits in a barber's shop, | As much in mock as mark*: Look like trivial penalties for minor transgressions, to be treated as a joke, rather than seriously respected. Barbers' shops are supposed to have hung up lists of penalties for swearing and similar minor offences among their customers (and cf. I.3.27).

330 *notedly*: Particularly.

332 *coward*: No such charge has hitherto been alleged against the Duke.

339 *close*: Compromise.

343 *bolts*: Fetters.

344 *giglots*: Harlots.

351 *sheep-biting face*: Lucio likens the Duke to the proverbial wolf in sheep's clothing, who employs the disguise in order to prey upon the flock.

   hanged: Hanging, the customary punishment for sheep-stealing, was extended to dogs and, in folk-lore, to other predatory animals.

360 *or . . . or . . . or*: Either . . . or . . . or.

367 *passes*: The various editorial glosses, for example, 'course of action', 'devices', 'events', are all plausible, but the tone of the whole passage suggests that Shakespeare intended the word to signify 'trespasses'.

380 *Advertising*: Attentive.

   holy: Devoted.

382 *Attorneyed*: Employed as an agent, or advocate for.

389 *remonstrance*: Revelation.

393 *brained*: Killed.

398 *salt*: Lecherous.

404 *The very mercy of the law*: Even the most merciful elements within the law.

405 *proper*: Very.

424 *definitive*: Immovable.

430 *sense*: Natural feeling.

431 *fact*: Crime.

432 *pavèd bed*: The implication is, presumably, that Claudio has been buried under the pavement of the prison.

450 *subjects*: People ruled over by a king or prince, members of a state.

461 *advice*: Reflection.

468 *still*: Always.

479 *And squar'st thy life according*: And pattern out your life accordingly.

480 *quit*: Acquit, pardon.

483 *muffled*: With his face hidden. It can also mean

'blindfold', but there is no obvious reason why Claudio should enter blindfold.

490 *But fitter time for that*: Dr Johnson and subsequent editors have been perturbed 'that Isabel is not made to express either gratitude, wonder or joy at the sight of her brother', but the Duke's insistence on a *fitter time* may explain why this is so. Shakespeare's comic denouement is sometimes made to sacrifice sentiment in the interests of technical dexterity. There is a sufficiently close parallel in *Cymbeline*, V.5.104–5, where Imogen dismisses her benefactor, Lucius, with the words: 'Your life, good master, | Must shuffle for itself.'

493 *quits*: Requites.

494 *her worth worth yours*: (Ensure that) you deserve her, that your worth lives up to hers.

495 *an apt remission*: A readiness to pardon.

498 *luxury*: Lechery.

501–2 *the trick*: My usual way of speaking, my joke (cf. III.2.49).

526 *more behind*: More to come.
      gratulate: Gratifying.

532 *motion*: Project.